THE LIFE OF IDA TARBELL

By Kate O'Dell

IDA TARBELL'S CHILDHOOD

Ida Minerva Tarbell was born on November 5th, 1857, in Hatch Hollow, Amity Township, Pennsylvania. Ida's mother was Esther Ann (née McCullough), who was a teacher. Her father was Franklin Summer Tarbell, who was also a teacher, and had worked as a joiner, and an oilman. She had three younger siblings – Walter, Franklin Jr., and Sarah. Franklin Jr. died very young of scarlet fever. Sarah also had scarlet fever, but she survived. Weakened by the disease, she later became an artist. Walter would go on to be an oilman like his father.

Esther had been born in Norwich, New York, and as a child, she'd moved to Pennsylvania with her father, Walter Raleigh McCullough, and her four siblings. He had remarried, then had another daughter after the move.

Esther had always been told about her heritage by her mother, which she passed on to her daughter. *'Remember that your father is a McCullough of an ancient and honoured Scotch clan, his mother a Raleigh of Sir Walter's family, that I am a Seabury, my great-uncle the first Episcopal bishop in the United States, my mother a Welles, her father on George Washington's staff.'* The genealogy lesson was passed down to her daughter, which Ida later wrote about in her autobiography.

Esther believed that women should have a proper education. In her youth, she had gone to boarding school at a Methodist female seminary, in Poughkeepsie, New York. She also went to a private school in Pennsylvania. By eighteen, Esther had graduated and went on to be a teacher. She taught a great deal of topics – geography, arithmetic, grammar, reading, and writing. At that time, only about fifty percent of women were able to read.

Her parents, Esther and Franklin, dated for six years before finally getting married on April 17, 1856. They were both twenty-six years old. Within their first year of marriage, Esther Tarbell got pregnant. The couple discussed their future in Hatch Hollow, Pennsylvania. It was a very small town – with only a school, a creamery, sawmill, and Methodist church. They thought that it would be better for their future child, to live in a better community.

They discussed the move to Iowa, trying to figure out what they wee going to do. Esther wouldn't have any income as a stay-at-home mother. If Franklin were to leave the state, she would become an 'economic dependant', and not entitled to any of his income, or property. But moving to Iowa seemed like the best option for the young couple.

In 1857, travel to Iowa would be difficult. They couldn't take the train, and a wagon trip was extremely difficult, especially for pregnant Esther. She feared leaving behind her family and friends, but wanted to be with her husband. And so it was decided, that Franklin would travel on his own to Iowa, and send for his wife when the homestead was ready.

Franklin believed that he could manage being on the road to Iowa. In his youth, he had worked piloting flatboats filled with cargo, travelling along the Ohio, Allegheny, and Mississippi Rivers. These trips were often in treacherous waters, stormy days, and meant that he'd had to survive on the small amount of food he'd brought aboard. He had had plenty of travel experience by the time he planned his trip to Iowa.

in 1857, Franklin left for Iowa, so he could build the family home. Iowa was much more economically safer than living in southern Pennsylvania. Iowa had only been a state for eleven years, and he hoped that the fertile soil would be a better farming choice for the family. Franklin Tarbell received farmer's income, as well as money from being a welder, and teacher.

Franklin's decision to move to another state was hardly unique. A great number of migrants were facing money troubles. People were moving out of states that supported slavery, and going to states that were more sympathetic to the abolition movement. Others, like Franklin Tarbell, felt restless, and needed to move on. Pennsylvania was not on the brink of starvation, and Tarbell's neighbours were bemused at his decision to leave. It is interesting to note, that even the Rockefeller family had moved from upstate New York, to Ohio in 1853. John D. Rockefeller had been fourteen years old at the time. Rockefeller was blissfully unaware of the Tarbell family at that time, but their futures were entwined, when Ida Tarbell would decide to write a scathing exposé about him and his oil company.

Franklin Tarbell successfully made the trip to Iowa, and picked out a plot of land that he thought would work well for his family. It was located in the southwest corner, north of the Missouri border. The federal government had been trying to entice settlers to move to Iowa, and also to the untouched land west of the Mississippi River. The government was selling the land at a cheap price – at $1.25 per acre. And at times, they were even giving away land for free (this was done as bounties for war veterans who were killing the Indigenous people, as the government hated anyone that was native, and preferred them dead so they could colonize their land). These genocidal bounties, as well as the land that the government sold for cheap, meant that there were about 36 million available Iowan acres, during the 1840s and 1850s.

Life in Iowa was difficult, as the new settlers had to deal with angry displaced Sioux, who fought back against the people who'd moved onto their land. There were some attacks, and the year that Franklin moved there, 34 settlers were killed in an attack (Spirit Lake Massacre). The settlers built tiny cabins, that were cramped and barely kept out the frigid winters. Their cabins were usually about 18x16 feet, and they had to huddle together to keep from getting frostbite, or dying. Sod houses weren't much warmer than the log cabins. It was an especially trying time for the settlers, as the land they lived on was freezing cold in winter, and was a harsh environment.

Franklin was eager to build his house, and so he got a job at the sawmill. He was then able to buy building supplies, while he built the house with his own hands. Franklin would write letters home, describing the flat Midwest land, the constant flow of settlers in wagons, his excitement for their new home. He had written to Esther, that he planned for her to hitch a wagon ride in August, travelling the hundreds of miles to their new home. Baby Ida was supposed to be born on the plains. But his plans fell through.

During the summer of 1857, the economy suffered greatly. It was dubbed '*the Panic of 1857*'. With the suffering economy, and the poor harvest season, the banks shut down – defaulting on individual accounts. Franklin Tarbell couldn't access his savings due to the banks collapsing. Cash was scarce. This left both Franklin, and Esther trapped by their lack of funds.

With so many settlers moving into the area, it had messed up the land market. Many settlers had bought more land than they had needed. With the farms getting mortgaged, and they were defaulting on their properties, the land was getting bought up by railroad companies, bankers, and others who were eager to buy the cheap land from the failing settlers. These companies profited greatly by buying up the land, despite the fact that these settlers were losing everything. For some, it was an inconvenience. For others, losing the land they had tried to settle on was a devastating blow.

On November 5th, Ida was born in a log cabin that belonged to her maternal grandfather, Walter Raleigh McCullough, and his wife. McCullough had been a Scottish-Irish pioneer. Ida's father's family had immigrated to New England in the 17th century. Ida had been told by her grandmother that their family was descended from Sir Walter Raleigh – the first American Episcopalian bishop, who had been in George Washington's staff. Ida, born on the cusp of the American civil war, was thrust into a tumultuous time.

By the time Ida was born, Franklin was still stuck in Iowa. Esther raised her daughter at her parent's place – a Cape Cod log cabin, with a wooden floor, with a large working fireplace in the living room, and was built with one and a half storeys. The property had pear and maple trees, and they had poultry, and a dairy farm. This helped the family live self-sufficiently, as Esther waited for her husband to return home.

With no access to his savings, and a great amount of workers being laid off, Franklin Tarbell knew that he had to leave Iowa behind. He needed to return home to Pennsylvania, to be with his wife and daughter. Penniless, he was forced to travel on foot – walking across Illinois, Indiana, and Ohio to return to his family. It took him eighteen months to finally return home, and Franklin had found work teaching in rural schools along the way.

When Franklin finally returned home, young Ida greeted him by saying *'Go away, bad man!'* She had been only eighteen months old, and had never met her father before. He was glad to be home. Eighteen months was an extremely long time to be away from his young wife, and the child he had yet to meet. Their reunion was bittersweet, glad to be home, and yet both mourning the loss of their Iowa home, and land.

Shortly after he returned home, Franklin revealed to Esther that he still planned on bringing his family to Iowa. Esther started to pack their stuff, and Franklin worked on a flatboat to get enough money for the move. But then something happened to the Tarbell's that disrupted their plans.

In August 1859, Franklin Tarbell was visiting with a friend, when they told him about a prospector near Titusville that had drilled for oil. Edwin L. Drake had discovered huge amounts of oil, which was incredibly valuable. This oil discovery would change the Tarbell family's money situation, and would provide employment for a great deal of interested prospectors.

For the remainder of the Tarbell's lives, they would be forever be connected to the oil industry. Both Franklin Tarbell, and his son Will

Tarbell, would become employed by the oil industry. And Ida Tarbell, who grew up in the Pennsylvania oil fields, and got to experience it first-hand, would eventually take on the corrupt Standard Oil Company, and the rich businessman behind it, John D. Rockefeller.

DRAKE OIL WELL

Titusville, Pennsylvania, was a rural lumber town with a great deal of pine and hemlock trees. Workers would float the logs down the Allegheny River, towards Pittsburgh. It was very rural, and not easily accessible.

Indigenous people, and geologists had long known that oil would occasionally seep out of the rocks, appearing in streams and shallows. The oil would create a film on top of the water, which could be ignited. There were some who believed that the oil had healing properties. They would skim the oil off the water's surface, and try to heal skin sores, or use it to heal damaged internal organs. Others would dip their wool blankets into the oil, then wring them out drop by drop to collect it.

A company called Seneca Oil, had used the oil in a *'cure for coughs, colds, and rheumatism'* – selling it in shops. Samuel M. Keir, entrepreneur from Pittsburgh, tried to sell the oil as *'Keir's Petroleum'*, or *'Rock-Oil'* – as a product that could be burned as a light source.

For the most part, the area was largely untouched by oil prospectors. Ebenezer Brewer, part owner for a lumber company outside of Titusville, insisted that they needed to skim the oil from the water, and sell it for a profit. He was curious about its properties, and so he sent off a sample to his son, Francis B. Brewer. Francis was a Vermont doctor, who had studied science. Francis tried out the substance on himself, and then on his patients. He determined that his father was on to something, and that the company could become quite rich selling the oil.

Brewer contacted New York lawyers, and made the Pennsylvania Rock Oil Company. In order for his company to extract large amounts of oil, they needed to do more than skim it off the water's surface. They would need to retrieve it from the underground. There were already salt miners, who would bring the oil up to the surface as a by-product. Considering it a nuisance, they would collect it in cisterns, and then discard it. With this knowledge, they were able to determine that underground extraction was possible.

Edwin Drake was hired by New York lawyers, and travelled to Titusville by train, and also stagecoach. He hired on a team of Titusville workers for manual labour. It took months to get the much-needed heavy equipment into the area, as they were dealing with wooden plank roads, and treacherous water. Drake had to make the trip multiple times from Titusville, to Pittsburgh, (which was a hundred miles distance), in search of a driller.

Drake was a man in poor health. Though he might not have been familiar with all of the tools needed, or their uses, he intuitively knew that they'd need to excavate further below the surface – at a depth further than had ever been attempted. In order to perfect the business, Drake needed to rely on trial and error, until he got things right.

Drake had not earned a great reputation around Titusville. Some saw him as a dreamer, others thought he was a lunatic. He had an incredibly hard time finding labourers, and an even harder time keeping them in his employ. Despite his poor reputation, Drake refused to give up.

Drake and his team had been working on breaking through the earth for months without any luck. Drake's attempts had been dubbed '*Drake's Folly*', for their lack of results. All of that changed, however, during the spring of 1859, when Drake and his workers finally achieved their mission.

Financial backers had stated that they would be pulling their funding. Drake said the following: '*You all feel different from what I do. You all have your legitimate business which has not been interrupted by the operation, which I staked everything I had upon the project and now fond myself out of business and out of money.*'

He was determined to see his project succeed, knowing that once he did manage to access the oil, everything would change for the better. And on August 27, 1859, Drake's drilling equipment struck oil. It was 70 feet below the surface, and the oil became known as *'black gold'*. Onlookers were shocked by what they saw, surprised at the force which the oil shot up out of the ground.

Two weeks later, the *New York Tribune* published an article about Drake's oil well, from a correspondent called Medicus. He had finally managed to reach the remote Titusville, and was excited to learn about the large amount of oil. Its discovery was being compared to California gold. Many believed that the oil discovery was a blessing from God, while others were extremely proud that their state had been the one to be bestowed with such riches.

Jonathan Watson was considered one of the first people to fully realize just how much money could be made from the oil well. Watson travelled to Titusville on horseback, visiting 43 different Titusville landowners. He had realized that the creeks, and lowland areas were the best areas to collect the oil. Instead of offering to buy out all the landowners, Watson instead asked them to lease him a portion of their land. Three weeks later, Watson became the largest leaseholder on Oil Creek. It was an expensive gamble, but one that turned out well for him.

Prospectors weren't concerned about damage to the environment in the slightest. Setting up their own oil well was relatively cheap, and so that's what they did. Many of them ultimately failed. And when they did, the failed prospectors often left behind a disgusting mess of uncapped wells, polluted soil and water, and the remains of their mining camps strewn about the land. This scenario played out repeatedly, as black gold became the next big boom.

It was an opportune time for the oil business. For years, companies had been capturing whales, and hauling them back home. Whale oil had been used as a light source. But whaling was a difficult endeavor, and the whale populations were in decline due to the nearly 700 ships scouring the sea for their prey. This raised the price of whale oil, making it difficult for middle class and lower-class families to afford it.

Some people started to use camphene – oil that was created from turpentine resin, from pine trees. It sold well enough, but transportation was difficult for areas that didn't have lots of pine trees. There were other light sources at the time. Members of the pork industry had created lard oil, in hopes that it would become popular. But lard oil had a really bad odour, and it became quite smoky.

Kerosene started to be a viable replacement for turpentine, lard oil, and whale oil. It was extracted from coal tar, and shale oil. Kerosene burned for a long time, which households enjoyed. But it was still more expensive than whale oil. There were also safety issues with the kerosene, as it clogged up lamps, and weren't very safe for confined spaces.

But Kerosene could also be extracted from petroleum. And this seemed like a better alternative. The Drake oil well would be an excellent source for this much needed oil. There was another reason why the oil would be in such high demand – and that was the factories. They wanted to keep their lights on for longer, so the workers could continue producing materials well into the night. And they would need to lubricate their machines.

As an adult, Ida Tarbell wrote a great deal about the oil industry, and in particular about Drake's oil well. It was considered such a huge discovery at the time, and Tarbell described its location as '*a sacred spot*'. She wrote the following passage about Drake's well: '*Here we have demonstrations of the enterprise and resourcefulness of American men in adapting what they knew to unheard-of industrial problems, of their patience and imagination in adding by invention, by trial and error, a body of entirely new mechanical and commercial devices and processes.*'

The Tarbell family was able to get back on their feet, with the Pennsylvania oil rush that began in 1859. The economy began to thrive with new oil fields blossoming up in the western area of Pennsylvania. The oil fields were able to give people much-needed employment. In her early years, Ida became acquainted with the Pennsylvania oil fields. This experience would later come in handy when she wrote about labour practises, and the Standard Oil Company. Later, in her autobiography, Ida Tarbell wrote the following: 'Oil opened a rich field for tricksters, swindlers, exploiters of vice in every known form'.

Franklin didn't immediately jump into the oil business. He studied it, seeing how people bought up or leased land in a frenzy, determined to get their share of the fortune. People were greedy, were honing in on the oil well. Franklin thought that it would be a good idea for him and Esther to put their Iowa plans aside for awhile, and join the throng of oil workers. It was much closer to home, and seemed a viable way for him to make good money. Iowa would still be there in a few months' time, or a few years. He'd need to act fast, if he wanted in on the initial rush at the oil field.

He decided to visit Titusville, which was a one-day trip from Hatch Hollow. Franklin was able to see firsthand the busy and industrious attempts at oil excavation, and the people clamouring to get to the top. While he was there, Franklin Tarbell was struck with inspiration. He would produce wooden oil storage tanks.

The oil well was in dire need of containers. When the oil well first opened up, Drake had not realized just how much oil they would be collecting. One of the first containers they had used, was a bathtub. Some would collect the oil in empty whiskey barrels. A local carpenter had collected pine boards from the sawmill, and then created vats for the oil well. Still, they were always desperate for more containers.

Barrel makers stepped up, and created barrels that could be shipped out. Until they could be shipped out, oilmen had made a wooden tank caulked with oakum, that was held together with iron loops. These wooden tanks were not the best at storing oil, as they often leaked.

In a single tank, the oilmen could store about a thousand barrels. There was a much higher demand, however. The market was demanding more than 10,000 barrels. These barrels didn't always stack properly, and were often made in different sizes – anywhere from 38-50 gallons. But as Franklin Tarbell stepped in, he created a 42-gallon standard, which was the same size as those used for whale oil in New England.

Before 1859, there really wasn't a huge demand for barrel making in the United States. Items such as whiskey, molasses, and turpentine had been shipped out in barrels, but they were made locally for the respective businesses. But with Drake's Well, there was a massive need for these oil barrels. The railroad expansion had been growing exponentially, which made it easier to ship out the oil barrels around the nation – and in some cases, even shipped overseas.

Franklin Tarbell brought forth his ideas for the storage proposal, explaining it to the oil drillers. He was well versed in his welding and carpentry skills. His blueprints won them over, and a group of drillers pooled their money together to pay for his barrels.

Within a few months, Franklin had hired on a large group of men, and they worked all hours creating the barrels. He needed to buy thousands of feet of lumber. His business thrived, and he would continue to work within the oil industry.

The more business he got, and the more hours he had to put in, Franklin had to spend less time with his family. He decided that they ought to move from Hatch Hollow, and live closer to the oil well. Ida was no longer his only child. She now had a younger brother, Walter William.

In October 1860, the Tarbells moved to Rouseville, so they would be close to his job. Their newly-built house, had a workshop for him to build the tanks. The oil field had 25 oil wells. It was everywhere – in the pits, sand, and puddles. It took three days to travel by horse-drawn lumber cart, to get from Titusville, to Rouseville.

Rouseville had been a very quiet town, about as isolated as Hatch Hollow. But in early 1860, Henry R. Rouse opened the first oil well in the town, inspired by the Drake Well. That changed everything in the area.

Rouse had been a lawyer and teacher, and he also realized just how much the oil would be worth. Fearing that the oil boom would bring crime to his small town, Rouse made sure to put down rules. When people leased land, Rouse told them that if anyone purchased or consumed alcohol, they would be forfeiting their lease. He didn't want any alcohol-fuelled violence on the land.

"*No industry of man,*" Ida Tarbell wrote, '*in its early days has ever been more destructive of beauty, order, decency, than the production of petroleum*'.

Life in Rouseville was a difficult life, and Ida witnessed several traumatizing workplace injuries that greatly impacted her. On April 17, 1861, Henry Rouse, neighbour and founder of Rouseville, had been drilling for oil. When a flame accidently hit natural gas coming from a pump, it sparked a massive oil well fire. Eighteen men were killed that day, with thirteen injured.

Severely injured, Rouse only survived for a few more hours. Before his death, he left half of his million-dollar estate to building roads, and bridges in Warren County. The rest of it went to his friends, and to building the *Rouse Home* in Youngsville. He died shortly after.

One of the reasons why this terrible explosion occurred, was because Rouse wanted to dig further than the standard 150 feet. Instead, he instructed them to dig at 300 feet. The drill hit an underground natural gas pocket, that also contained crude oil. It created a huge amount of pressure, and the oil shot up 60 feet into the air. They were shockingly allowed to collect about 3,000 barrels each day.

Rouse was determined to keep the workplace safe, knowing that they needed to maintain special care with the large amount of oil. But the workers were not as safety oriented. It was believed that a spark (likely from a lamp, or match), started the fire, which led to the explosion.

One of the survivors was George H. Dimick. He remembered that '*an acre of ground with two wells, and their tankage, a barn and a large number of barrels of oil were in flames*'.

Other workers who had seen the explosion, described it as '*the flow of oil enveloped in a sheet of flame which extended far above their heads, and which was fed by the oil thrown upon their clothing by the explosion*.'

After the explosion, Franklin Tarbell hurried to the explosion site, and tried to help as many people as he could. Families were grieving, and the area was terrible shape. When he finally came back home, Franklin was exhausted, and fell into bed. It wasn't long after, that someone knocked on their door. The man, an acquaintance of theirs, was severely burned all over his body. For weeks, Esther took care of him, trying to nurse him back to health. Eventually, he got better, and was able to leave their house.

Ida Tarbell recalled years after the incident, the smell of linseed oil, which Esther had spread over the man's burned skin. The oil would come off onto the sheets and pillows, staining them permanently – no matter how many times the bedding was laundered.

Despite Rouse's death, especially in such a gruesome fashion, workers continued to drill for oil. They seemed unconcerned with the fact that some of them may die or get injured like the unfortunate workers.

There were two miners, Cyrus D. Phipps and Walter Whann, who were working on tightening the hoops on a storage tank near one of the oil wells. They were nearly finished their task, when the tank burst. It had held thousands of barrels of oil, and it threw Whann onto the floor several yards away. Phipps was thrown in the opposite direction, into the oil. He found himself lying in a pile of wreckage, body battered, his clothes ripped off his body. They both survived, and Phipps went on to continue working on the oil well site.

There had been another incident, where three women had died in a kitchen explosion. Though Ida had not been allowed to see the gruesome bodies, she later snuck into the room, and saw the women laid out in preparation for their burial. Ida had been extremely young, and the sight of the women's burned bodies terrified her. She was plagued with nightmares for the remainder of her life.

The move from Hatch Hollow, to Rouseville was a difficult one for young Ida Tarbell. She missed living in the log cabin with her parents, and grandparents. She missed the beautiful trees and flowers, and the farm animals on the property. It had been an idyllic place to grow up, with plenty of fresh air, and nature. A place she could run around, and play.

Their new family home was crowded, with the children's room filled with trundle beds. The town was always covered in muck, and the water was always covered in a thin sheen of oil. Always the constant drilling, and overcrowded conditions. All local plant life were dying, covered in tar and oil. There was always the threat of Ida and Will being injured or killed with all the machinery, and oil wells surrounding their home, and the constant threat of explosions, or fires. Esther kept her children indoors for the most part, always having them within reach. It was a far cry from the small log cabin where Ida had been born, and she struggled to feel comfortable in her new surroundings.

Tarbell wrote about the sudden change of environment. '*My rebellion didn't come from natural depravity; on the contrary, it was a natural and righteous protest against having the life and home I had known, and which I loved, taken away without explanation and a new scene, a new set of rules which I did not like, suddenly imposed.*'

It was a dangerous place to raise children, and there were very few activities for them to enjoy. Esther became stressed out, and incredibly fearful that her two young children would cross the footbridge over the stream, and drown in the oil storage pits near the family home.

Ida loved to explore, and she was always rebelling against her mother. One day, she wanted to experiment with flotation. She went down to the brook, and studied it. It was swelling, nearly flooding. Ida, always the little scientist, decided to toss a few small items into the water, and see what would happen. She discovered that some items would float on the surface, while others would sink.

Ida wondered what would happen if she dropped her baby brother into the water. She wondered if Will, bundled up in all of his toddler dresses, would sink or float? It was a question that stayed on Ida's mind for some time. The next time that her mother was out, Ida took her young brother to the foot bridge, and dropped him into the water. Will was wearing a great deal of skirts and dresses, and these clothing saved him. The material spread out, enough to keep him from drowning. A workman nearby heard Will screaming, and jumped into the swelling brook to pull him out. Ida recalled being punished for her science experiment, and also came away with the knowledge that her brother could be categorized as something that would float. The experiment was clearly dangerous, but it was indicative of her curiosity, and constant need to study the world around her. She had had a hypothesis, and needed to perform her science experiment to understand what would happen.

In later years, Franklin Tarbell would be an oil producer, and refiner in Venango County. The Tarbell family would be permanently enmeshed with the American oil industry, from Franklin's years of experience, to Ida Tarbell's eventual articles about Rockefeller, and the Standard Oil Company.

TITUSVILLE

In 1870, the Tarbell family moved to Titusville. It was a booming oil town, with railroad track laid out the year beforehand. Eleven years before, when Franklin had first found out about Drake's Well, Titusville had a very small population of only 300. But by 1870, the population of Crawford County had reached nearly 63,000.

She was almost thirteen by the time Ida moved to Titusville. She liked the new town a lot more than the oil-drenched Rouseville. Even after she moved to New York, and Connecticut, Ida Tarbell would always consider Titusville her hometown. It was a much more civilized place compared to the rugged, polluted atmosphere. Franklin had decided to close down his Pithole shop, as it was hemorrhaging money. The Pithole wells were no longer profitable.

Titusville, was named after Johnathan Titus – who had worked for the Dutch Holland Land Company. He had showed up in 1796, though the town wasn't technically created until 1809. It was incorporated as a borough in 1847, which easily predated the discovery of oil in the area. Titusville was not just an oil town. It also had other industries – such as lumber, coal, etc. They were more refined than places like Rouseville. They had their own police force, had drains, and sewer systems, and their wooden walkways reduced the mud. Residents didn't have to slog through knee-high mud like in Rouseville. Titusville had about a dozen churches, a decent education system, and even had gas lights set up near the roads.

When the Tarbells decided to move to Titusville, they bought two lots on Main Street. It cost them a total of $1,000. Their new house was located at 324 East Main Street, and stood out because of its beautiful architecture.

In 1866, a Pithole hotel called the Bonta House, posted that they would be hosting a distress sale. Their business was going under, and they'd be selling off furniture, as well as other fixtures. Franklin bought the hotel for $600 (even though it had once been valued at $60,000). He then ripped out any salvageable materials that he needed for his new house (woodwork, French windows, iron brackets, etc.), and had them shipped the ten miles to Titusville. When he had removed everything of value, Franklin Tarbell had the defunct hotel property torn down. He used those resources, incorporating them into his newly-built family home. Big enough for him, his wife, and their children to live comfortably.

The Tarbell family were very socially active. They would often invite women suffragist guests, and prohibitionists into their house. Esther Tarbell was deeply invested in women's rights, and would entertain woman such as Mary Livermore, and Frances E. Willard. Willard was a woman's suffragist, and educator, who spent her life focused on reform systems. She raised the age of consent in multiple states, and passed labour reforms such as the eight-hour workday.

The Tarbells considered themselves a well-read family. They subscribed to *Harper's Weekly, Harper's Monthly*, and *The New York Tribune*. Ida Tarbell would read these publications with vigour, following the events of the Civil War. She would also sneak into the worker's bunkhouse, and read editions of *The Police Gazette,* a gruesome tabloid.

They were a Methodist household, and they attended church twice a week. Ida Tarbell was an exceptionally bright student, but fared poorly in the classroom. Ida admitted that she didn't pay attention in class, and often skipped classes. She was not really used to being in class for so long, as she had been homeschooled before, or tutored in various people's houses with the other children in Rouseville. Her truancy stopped, after one of her teachers pulled her aside, and talked to her sternly about her behaviour.

Ida strived to become a better student, especially after she became interested in science, comparing her school lessons to the Pennsylvania landscape around her. Throughout her transient childhood, Ida had studied the natural world around her – plants, insects, and rocks. She had been prone to bringing home all sorts of rocks and small animals, often keeping them in bottles to study them further. It had been a fun childhood activity. But as she studied sciences in school, Ida discovered that school could actually be fun and interesting.

Ida graduated from high school on June 25, 1875. She had had a 99% grade average. Ida Tarbell was upset that she'd be leaving her parents to go to college, but she knew that it was for the best. She was a highly ambitious young woman, and eager to create change for the better.

ALLEGHENY COLLEGE

By the time she had graduated high school in Titusville, Ida Tarbell was at the top of her class. She had graduated with flying colours, with a 99% mark. After careful consideration, Ida Tarbell decided to attend Allegheny College in 1876, to study biology. Ida was the only female student, out of a class of forty-one.

Leaving home had been a difficult decision for Ida, as she longed to stay with her parents, and younger siblings. At the same time, however, Ida was determined to get an education. Armed with the knowledge that she needed to right the wrongs in the oil industry, and filled with an inquisitive nature, Ida Tarbell was determined to create change for the better. She was a fiercely independent woman, and wanted to prove her worth. Very few colleges accepted women at the time, but she was determined to get a college degree.

Ida Tarbell was deeply in love with evolutionary biology. As a child, she had had a microscope, and used it often. *'The quest for the truth had been born in me, the most essential of man's quests.'* Ida Tarbell wrote, about her love of science.

Tarbell had dreamed of attending Cornell University, which was located in Ithica, New York. The school had been for male students only, but in 1872, it had finally started accepting female students. She didn't attend Cornell, however. This was because Ida Tarbell was confronted by a man named Lucius Bugbee at her parents' home. Bugbee was a professor, minister, banker – and during his academic career he was president of schools for girls in Evanston, Cooperstown, and Cincinnati. He had recently been hired to run Allegheny College. It was thirty miles away from Titusville, located in Meadville, Pennsylvania.

Allegheny College was run by the Methodist church. Built in 1815, the school only started admitting female students in 1870. Matthew Simpson was the church's Allegheny faculty member, who supported women's rights, and the suffrage movement.

Esther Tarbell had hoped to attend Allegheny College in her youth, but she wasn't allowed to go, as they didn't take female students yet. She was excited at the prospect of her daughter attending the school. Franklin, however, was not nearly as excited as his wife. The tuition and other college expenses were too much for him, given that he had lost business recently. But Bugbee was a very convincing man, and he emphasized the school's merits, and how Ida would be only a short drive away. She could come home whenever she needed to.

'It was near home, it was a ward of our church,' Ida Tarbell said, on her decision to choose Allegheny over Cornell. 'It had responded to the cry of women for educational opportunity and had opened its doors before the institution I had chosen. Was not here an opportunity for a serious young woman interested in the advancement of her sex? Had I not a responsibility in the matter? If the few colleges that had opened their doors were to keep them open, if others were to imitate their example, two things were essential – women must prove they wanted a college education by supporting those in their vicinity, and they must prove by their scholarship what many doubted, that they had minds as capable of development as young men. Allegheny had not a large territory to draw from. I must be a pioneer.'

Firstly, Ida had to pass the entrance exams. She needed to prove her worth in Latin, Greek, modern languages, English grammar, history, natural philosophy, botany, geometry, algebra, and physiology.

There had been only nineteen female students in Allegheny, before Tarbell enrolled in 1876. Only two of those women had graduated. The male students had at first been against any women students in their school, claiming that it was now 'a blooming female seminary'.

When the first few female students attended the college, the faculty wives, and other staff members kept an especially careful eye on the women students, making sure they wore appropriate clothing that was unattractive, to get less attention from the male students. The female students were not to laugh too loudly, flirt with the boys, or even glance their way. They were not to chat with their male classmates after their lessons, and were kept strictly in line.

To get to the college, Tarbell needed to travel for a full day. First, she would travel either by train, or by carriage – as she needed to switch trains at Corry. She needed somewhere to stay, but the school dorms were only for male students. This caused her some difficulty, as she needed to find someone to take her in. Tarbell stayed at different faculty wives' houses, and at one point, even stayed with President Bugbee and his wife. Though everyone was pleasant to her, and she appreciated their hospitality, Tarbell wanted to have a permanent place to stay.

One of her favourite professors, was Ammi B. Hyde, who taught English, and the classics. She found him to be quite entertaining, and he was highly intelligent. Although she loved his teaching style, Tarbell recalled being intimidated by him – as many of the female students were. Hyde lived large, knowing a great deal about the Greeks, Latins, and all sorts of philosophers. Tarbell became friends with Hyde's wife, and daughter, but still she felt never truly comfortable.

And then the school finally created a women's dormitory. The building was painted white, and dubbed 'The Snowflake'. It was for Allegheny's female students, as well as the few who had enrolled in the nearby prep school. It faced the back of Culver Hall (the men's dormitory).

Curfew was at 10 PM. School staff had a difficult time getting the students to abide by the curfew, and there were occasions when male students would sneak into the Snowflake to visit their classmates. Tarbell wasn't one to normally associate with her male classmates. It was partially because she was quite shy around them. But there was always the fear of expulsion, in case any of the teachers accused her of impropriety. Her need for education overshadowed any relationship she might have with a male classmate.

During her sophomore year, Tarbell and twenty other students moved from the 'Snowflake' building, to 'Black Maria'. It was in poor shape, and not fit for student housing. Allegheny quickly became aware that it wasn't a good fit for them, and started to look for a different housing situation. The school purchased 'Bunce House' – a group of small houses that were connected to one another. Tarbell's room was on the first floor, with a small side window. It allowed her to not only watch the comings and goings of her female classmates, but allowed her to sometimes see the male classmates as they visited the building in secret. Tarbell thrived in college. She was madly in love with the architecture, such as Bentley Hall. She had never seen such beautiful buildings before. And studying at the college meant that she could focus on her lessons, as well as learning as much as she could about current events. But her absolute favourite part of the college, was the library. It was well stocked with the Bentley collection, as well as valuable books such as the ones from Judge James Winthrop, of Cambridge, Massachusetts. She found comfort among the stacks, given free reign of the massive collection.

Many of the female students made a point to downplay their appearances, already quite conspicuous on campus for being women. A lot of them felt uncomfortable with the looks people gave them as they walked to class, some in curiosity, others displeased with women being in their school. Tarbell decided to that she needed to own it. If her classmates wanted to look, let them look. She was tall at 5'8", and stood out like a sore thumb. Esther Tarbell helped her daughter design, and sew her clothes. Some of them were quite eye-catching.

Tarbell recalled wearing a particular outfit in her freshman year, that was '*a tightly fitting black alpaca redingote, down to my instep in front, a tiny train behind. It was trimmed with forty-eight white pearl buttons*'.

Tarbell had worn it with a scarlet felt petticoat, as well as black silk scallops. She had been forced to lift the hem of her dress while walking on the uneven ground, and soon a great deal of faculty and classmates had learned about the colour of her petticoat.

From the beginning, Tarbell knew that there were certain sections of the school where she would not be allowed to frequent, simply because she was a woman. She felt like an invader, never completely sure of the rules or taboos that were to be respected with the different genders present on the same campus. There were some rules that were staunchly followed, but other rules were not posted. They were the unsaid sort, that Tarbell struggled with.

There was one time that Tarbell recalled, where she had left class, and decided to sit under a tree to find some shade. One of the seniors were quick to inform her that she was not to sit in that area, as it was only for men. There were other occasions where these undeclared rules, and social rules were not clearly stated, and got her into an uncomfortable situation.

One of her professors, Jeremiah Tingley, was an inquisitive man who had taught at a few different schools before becoming Allegheny faculty. Tingley and his wife occasionally invited Tarbell over for dinner of venison, or duck. They were a childless couple, who had travelled all over the globe. The Tingley couple lived in part of Bentley Hall, along with their great collection of items they had amassed from their trips abroad. They encouraged her to find enjoyment in her lessons, as opposed to many of the more conservative, Puritanical teachers.

Tingley granted Ida Tarbell time away from the classroom, so she could attend the 1876 Centennial Exposition. Ida and Franklin travelled to Fairmount Park, Philadelphia, alongside the Schuylkill River. It was a massive event, spread out over two hundred acres. There were more than 30,000 exhibits, in 167 buildings.

Ida Tarbell was truly impressed with everything that she saw. One area that caught her eye, was the Woman's Building, which featured *the results of woman's labours*. There were countless exhibits showcasing all sorts of scientific breakthroughs and inventions. Tarbell got to see the Corliss steam engine, which was powered by separate intake, and exhaust valves for each cylinder. She was truly at home, getting to witness the future of science unfolding in front of her eyes.

After Tarbell returned to Allegheny, Tingley was greatly interested in everything that she had seen. One of the inventions he was interested in, was the Telephone. It had only been a few months, since Asa Gray, and Alexander Graham Bell had done demonstrations to show just how the telephone worked, and how it could be a life-changing invention. It could change how people communicated all over the globe, able to connect family, friends, and people from other continents.

Unfortunately, Tarbell had not attended that exhibit. She listened to her teacher explain in great deal to the class just how important he believed the telephone was, and how he hoped to buy telephone stocks. Tarbell thought that he was a dreamer. She didn't see the same potential in the new invention that Tingley did.

Tingley soon discovered that Ida Tarbell had a love for microscopes. Enthused, he allowed Ida the use of the college's microscope. She carefully collected samples of the Common Mudpuppy, a foot-long amphibian from the local stream. Using the school's binocular-style microscope, Tarbell studied the mudpuppies, thinking that the foot-long creatures might be the missing link on the evolutionary chain. This was because the amphibian used both lungs and gills to breathe, as they lived in mud, and water. This love of microscopes was something she would continue to enjoy for her entire lifetime.

She was still terribly shy around male classmates, but Tarbell found herself quite interested in them. By age eighteen, she had hardly ever spent time with guys her own age. There had been a few crushes over the years, but she had never gone up and spoken to them.

But despite her casual interest in male classmates, it is unknown whether she actually sought out romance. She was uncomfortable with the idea of falling in love. Ida had long said that she was never going to marry, or have children. And she hated the idea of being a housewife, tending to the household instead of working. None of that appealed to her.

There were occasions, however, when Fraternity members would offer her their pins. She always felt uncomfortable, never knowing just how to handle the situation. She resented that they would 'tag' her, and instead preferred to have friends in all of the fraternities.

She recalled one morning, when she had gone into chapel wearing four different fraternity pins on her coat. She was considered a social outcast for a few months, having broken social rules in the school. Accepting and wearing the pins were, for many, similar to wearing a boyfriend's letterman jacket, or promise ring. Tarbell had had to stick to her few non-fraternity friends (mainly her female classmates), as the other classmates wanted nothing to do with her for a while. It had been a difficult time, as Tarbell had not realized that something as small as wearing multiple pins on her coat could be considered such an atrocity. Thankfully, during her sophomore year, there were seven new female students enrolled in the freshman class. Tarbell was able to befriend some of them, and life resumed as normal.

While she studied at Allegheny, Ida Tarbell involved herself greatly with school activities. She was a founding member of the sorority, that became the Mu chapter of the Kappa Alpha Theta sorority in 1876. She also had a sophomore stone placed on campus, that was dedicated to learning. It was inscribed with the Latin phrase '*Spes sibi quisque*', which means '*Everyone is his/her own hope*', although Tarbell preferred the translation '*Your hope lies within*'.

Ida was also a member of the women's literary society – *the Ossoli Society*. It was named after author Margaret Fuller Ossoli, who wrote for the society's publication '*The Mosaic*'. Previously, the Mosaic had been an all-male publication, but that soon changed. The Ossoli society had been created, after two literary societies (*the Allegheny*, and the *Philo-Franklin*) would meet regularly for debates, and study parliamentary procedure. But that was only for male students. Tarbell, not to be left out, decided to form a literary society where she could actively participate with her female classmates.

The Ossoli Society would invite the male students for their annual formal gathering (it was a chaperoned event by faculty members). Tarbell preferred the female-only events. During these, some of the women would opt to wear the male clothing. Tarbell herself participated in this fashion, at one point arriving to the event in her brother's military outfit.

Tarbell was convinced that she shouldn't pick one single thing to excel at – science, public speaking, writing, etc. No, she thought it best to excel at everything she could in college.

During her senior year oration, Tarbell spoke out in favour of Charles Dicken's writing, as he wrote about human nature, and empathy. Romantic fiction, however, was a genre that Tarbell disliked. She called it '*a grotesque collection of fancies*'.

She enjoyed the Ossoli society a great deal, as it gave her and the other students the opportunity '*for free discussion and free exercise of whatever little talent we might have as writers*'. Tarbell researched extensively the life and writing career of Elizabeth Barret Browning. '*Sometimes*', she discovered, '*fame was bestowed on those who never sought it – even women in a male-dominated society*'. Tarbell thought this was quite interesting, and gave her a sliver of hope that perhaps, she could have a bigger impact than regular people.

After Ida Tarbell had completed her presentation on Elizabeth Barret Browning, there was an article in the campus newspaper that summed it up in the following passage: '*She showed that our present results had been brought about by toil and perseverance. That to every age had been entrusted something to develop whose light has been the peculiar work of that period. She spoke of the great interest manifested in women's education, and how variously this subject has been viewed in the ages. She touched a chord in every true man or woman's heart when she said* 'teach woman that she must be educated, not for man, but for her Creator."

Ida Tarbell graduated in 1880 with an A.B degree, and then with an M.A degree in 1883. She later served on the school's board of trustees, after being elected in 1912. Ida was the second ever woman to serve as a trustee, and held that position for more than thirty years.

TEACHING AT POLAND, OHIO

After graduating, Ida Tarbell needed to decide what she was going to do. She wanted to contribute to society, but was unsure how to go about it. In 1880, it was considered standard practise for many college-educated women to go into teaching school. Before graduation, she had never really considered any other options. She wanted to make a difference, to change the world for the better. Tarbell was an eager student, an idealistic young woman.

During her senior year at college, Tarbell received a visit from a committee, looking to hire a teacher. They were from a Presbyterian private school, in Poland, Ohio. It was near the Pennsylvania border, a full day's ride from her parents' home.

Tarbell decided to take the teaching position. In August 1880, she started her new position as headmistress, at the Poland Union Seminary, in Poland, Ohio. The school taught high school, and it also taught continuing education courses for local teachers. Ida Tarbell taught a variety of subjects: geometry, geology, botany, trigonometry, German, French, Greek, and Latin. It was a great deal of work for a first-time teacher, and she struggled to keep up.

At first, she enjoyed her teaching position. Tarbell enjoyed Poland, Ohio. It was a quaint village, with deep roots and culture. It was quiet, unperturbed by the sounds of railroads, coal or iron factories that were nearby. There were a great deal of cottages and houses, farmland dotted with sheep, and horses. The seasons were marked by harvests. It was a beautiful sort of place for her to work, as she loved nature.

But after two years, Ida became burnt out by the heavy workload. Tarbell hadn't been fully informed about her teaching position, and how difficult it would be. She was to take over from Miss Blakelee, who was retiring. The faculty, the students, and the parents were all quite fond of Blakelee, believing that she could do no wrong. With Tarbell taking over the position, she had big shoes to fill. A lot of the staff and parents weren't as receptive towards the new teacher.

Miss Blakelee's reputation continued to follow Tarbell. People were quick to remind her that her predecessor had taught generations of Poland's residents. Children, parents, they had all looked up to the elderly teacher. Tarbell, on the other hand, was considered green, fresh-faced. Inexperienced. They disliked this about her, and made it known.

As time went on, it became quite apparent that she needed extra assistance. Tarbell confronted the seminary president, asking for help in her classroom. Her request was denied. The president limited his role to '*conducting the chapel with more or less grandiloquent remarks*'. Unhelpful.

She finally decided to quit, as she was barely getting paid enough to get by. It had come to a point where she had had to borrow money from her parents. Though her teaching career was a short one, it gave her the skills going forward to multi-task, and organizing lessons for each separate subject would aid in her future career as a nonfiction writer.

Life in Poland, Ohio would affect her in another way. Tarbell would eventually use this sort of community, and others, as examples in her muckraking articles. Poland had been an agricultural town, which soon became overcome by the oil industry, the iron mills, the coal mines. She wrote about the changes Poland went through with these industries moving in. '*The iron mills and coal mines brought the destruction of beauty, the breaking down of standards of conduct, the growth of the love of money for money's sake, the grist of social problems facing the countryside form the inflow of foreigners and the instability of work*.'

Poland had begun to change for the worse, as they brought in more industry, relying less on the agriculture of before. Slum houses had begun cropping up in Poland, and nearby Youngstown, and with it, less reputable people. There was also the issue of unsafe factory conditions, with one particular incident leaving workers burned to death after the furnace blew up, and flung molten metal over them.

For the two years that she spent in Poland, Ohio, Tarbell had been kept extremely busy, her hectic schedule leaving very little time for science experiments, or any time with her microscope. This was greatly upsetting, as it was her passion.

She decided to return to Pennsylvania, back to Titusville. Tarbell was twenty-four years old, and jobless. She kept herself busy. Tarbell took care of her ageing maternal grandfather, who had recently lost his wife. She cared for the property, helping with chores and repairs. For a while, she became active in the Titusville Shakespeare Club. Her younger brother had just had children of his own, and was busy working in the oil industry. Instead of joining forces with Rockefeller's Standard Oil Company, he had decided to work as an independent producer. Ida Tarbell helped care for her brother's children while she was in between jobs.

It was a time of great change. Her parents and brother were struggling to be successful as independent in the oil industry, as Rockefeller's Standard Oil Company continued to grow and grow, seizing up business left, right, and center. People were getting forced out of their jobs, trying to contend with the fact that Standard Oil was growing into a monstrous corporation.

Ida Tarbell had started to look into graduate schools, hoping to study biology. She still had a great deal of aspirations, and yearned to find her place in the world, but it was becoming more difficult.

In those days, twenty-five was the year that a woman would become an old maid, or spinster. No husband, no children, no job, and no wealth. Tarbell was struggling to come to terms with the fact that despite successfully getting through college, she had nothing to show for it. Her former life, filled with classes, and literary society gatherings was in the past.

It was commonplace that unmarried women would live with their parents. She loved her parents and younger siblings. But still, Ida Tarbell didn't see herself living with them for the remainder of her life. Being a stay-at-home daughter was boring, and mundane. Tarbell knew that she needed to figure something else out.

TARBELL'S NEW JOB AT THE CHAUTAUQUAN

It was at this point in her life, that Ida Tarbell met Theodore L. Flood. He was the editor of *The Chautauquan*, a teaching supplement for home study courses based out of Chautauqua, New York. The forty-year-old Methodist preacher would occasionally preach at the Tarbells' church. It was the sort of meeting that would change Ida Tarbell's life forever. Ida Tarbell had never considered being a writer, or working for a magazine. But when she met Flood, the idea sounded intriguing. It was something she could definitely do, as she had the perfect skill set for it.

Ida Tarbell was already moderately familiar with the Chautauqua self-improvement gatherings, as they had been part of her life since she'd been a teenager. Ida was interested in the adult education program, as she was a big fan of self-study.

The Chautauqua program had been created by Lewis Miller, a Methodist from Greentown, Ohio. He had been interested in expanding religious education outside of a Sunday school program. He had the idea of a *'family retreat'* where children and their parents could do their education from any location, while still keeping to their Christian beliefs. It would have *'a college without walls'* approach, one that meant adults could continue their education long after they graduated high school. Courses could be completed by having students learn for just one hour a day, for a total of nine months. And students could gather in 'circles', which were local discussion groups. These could be parents, siblings, neighbours, friends.

The very first ever educational gathering on the Chautauqua Lake shore, happened in August, 1874. Ida Tarbell had been seventeen at the time, and still in school – which was why she didn't attend straightaway. There were about five hundred in attendance, most of these were Sunday school teachers, mainly Methodist. They slept in tents, and attended lectures and concerts for a two-week period.

As it caught traction, mainly from word of mouth, Miller started to improve upon the area. Furnished lakeside cottages cropped up, ready to rent out to middle-class guests. The richer clientele could stay at the first-class Athenaeum Hotel. In 1875, Ulysses S. Granted visited the site, and journalists clamoured to report the Chautauqua story in their publications. The organizers made sure to keep the emphasis on education.

Ida Tarbell had attended one of the Chautauqua events, and eagerly listened as the lecturer spoke about their education program. Women and teenaged girls were their main clientele, as they would purchase books, and tests, and bring them home. They were spurred on by the women's rights movement, keen to get an education. They were determined to band together, and become self-taught through the education program.

In 1882, Theodore L. Flood had been invited over to the Tarbell home in Titusville. He had been working out of Jamestown, New York. But recently, he had moved the magazine to Meadville, as that was where the printing shop was located. It had a circulation of approximately 50,000. The Tarbells knew him from their church, as he occasionally attended, and had delivered a few guest sermons.

Throughout the night, Flood became increasingly aware that Ida Tarbell was brilliant, and was extremely familiar with the Chautauqua philosophy. He was looking to hire someone for editorial help, and thought that Tarbell would make a find addition to the magazine.

At first, Ida Tarbell had her doubts. She had never considered the possibility before, and it took a while for her to decide if that was where she wanted to go in her career. Ida was interested in earning a salary, and was interested in Flood's offer. She could work two weeks in

Meadville, and the other two weeks, she could stay with her parents and work on any microscope research she desired. This schedule especially pleased her, because she loved using the microscope. She had written the following: *Never had anything so thrilled me as chasing the protean amoeba. Never had I gloated over any achievement as discovering under the microscope the delicate foraminifera, and mounting them on slides.*

Tarbell took up Flood's offer. To her, it seemed a good temporary job, until she could find something more to her liking. He put in a short introduction into the magazine, announcing that Tarbell would be joining the team.

One of Tarbell's new Chautauqua jobs, was to help readers understand the books that they had read, from the Chautauqua Literary and Scientific Circle. Ida would proofread, and answer reader's questions about proper pronunciation of certain words. She would also translate foreign phrases, define words, and identify characters. A great many of their readers lived in rural settings and small communities. They had no home dictionaries, or encyclopedias. Many of them were hours away from a library, and were having a difficult time understanding the books they were working on. The magazine started to add some of the book texts into the magazine, complete with annotations, to aid their readers. Tarbell recalled that in her childhood, she knew that some households would only possess a Bible, and some children's spellers. Books always came after bread, and people often didn't have time to read for pleasure, after working long hours.

She became obsessed with getting every page proofread, worried that she might mistakenly put an accent in the wrong place, or submit a wrong birth year for someone in the magazine. Tarbell scoured over reference materials, realizing that she would soon need access to more updated reference materials.

Tarbell started to stay in Meadville more often, so she could access the Allegheny College library on a regular basis. Sometimes, this meant crashing in Flood's guest room overnight. This arrangement later changed to Tarbell sharing a house with her female colleagues from the Chautauqua magazine. The group were all extremely hard workers, putting in long hours. They rarely stayed at the house, and ended up paying the mother of one of the tenants to clean the house while they were at work. Tarbell was able to contribute by cooking, though she had only mastered a few recipes. She made excellent pie crusts, waffles, and Scotch woodcock. But other than that, her cooking was average.

Though Tarbell had only intended on joining the magazine on a temporary basis, she refused to phone it in. As was her nature, Tarbell always put a hundred percent effort into her work – which was more than could be said about Theodore Flood. He was never detail-oriented, and the magazine suffered from his disorderly approach. Tarbell instantly tried to create change for the better, maintaining the office space, while focusing on her magazine articles, and letters from avid readers.

Flood's system had pre-formatted letters made up, which was something that bothered Tarbell immensely. A great deal of the letter-writers, were women who needed counsel on matters, while also seeking out understanding, and empathy. Tarbell tried her best to respond to the letters with the perfect amount of sympathy, and empathy that she saw fit, giving the women a positive role model to lean on for support.

Tarbell decided to take up Flood's letter-writing, so that she could offer better advice for her readers. Flood seemed unaware of this change for months, even though she had been signing his name on the letters. It was only when a male colleague visited the magazine, and expressed gratitude towards his understanding attitude in his recent letters, that Flood went and checked the recent publications. He realized what had been going on. The colleague became upset when he realized that it was actually Tarbell – a woman – who was behind the recent letters, and he quickly left the Meadville office in disgust. After that, Tarbell declined from writing any more letters.

In 1885, Tarbell started to question her *Chautauqua* job. She felt that her role at the magazine was only have a very minimal role in the world, and thought that perhaps it was time to move on. She lamented in her journal, that it was difficult to work at the magazine, as many of her male colleagues, most of them being forty or older, would often hit on the women – and give them compliments based on their appearance, instead of their intelligence.

She was still editing articles, and working on minor projects. But at that time, she was not supposed to be writing articles. There were very few magazines, or newspapers that would hire women journalists to work on serious articles. Flood wanted to keep Tarbell on in the magazine, and so he started to let Tarbell work on small assignments. She started to write for a column titled 'Editor's Note Book'.

Ida Tarbell also started to write small articles for the magazine, which allowed her to find her writing voice. Slowly, she worked her way up to longer features. In December 1886, her first article was published. It was titled '*The Arts and Industries of Cincinnati*'. The article was about the city's various industries, as well as the interesting culture and arts scene in the city. Tarbell made a point to mention donations used to create the arts school, music hall, and museum. She had visited the city first-hand, to understand as much of Cincinnati's scene as she could. This meant actually meeting residents, and getting to visit the beer factory in person, and understanding what made Cincinnati stand out. Tarbell's article was successful, and well-received, and it led her to work on other great articles over time.

Steve Weinberg, from '*Taking on the Trust*', believed that that was when Tarbell had truly established her writing style, one that she would continue to use throughout the remainder of her career. Weinberg said the following: '*Tarbell would imbue her articles, essays, and books with moral content, grounded in her unwavering rectitude. That rectitude, while sometimes suggesting inflexibility, drove her instincts for reform, a vital element in her future confrontation with Rockefeller.*'

Tarbell had created a specific methodology when it came to her writing. First and foremost, was '*work, and work hard*'. Tarbell had had an early interest in science, and she often used the scientific processes in her writing, using hypothesis, and then seeking out all the pertinent evidence to support her theories. She immersed herself in as much evidence as possible, to the point where some critics have described her early works as '*drowning in facts*'. She always kept her work professional, with a scholarly approach to the fast-paced magazine deadlines. As well as working on her articles and books, Tarbell would also dictate about twenty letters per day, from her '*To Be Answered*' pile on her desk.

In March 1887, her article '*Women as Inventors*' was published in *The Chautauquan*. Ida had read an article written by Mary Lowe Dickinson, claiming that there were only three hundred women patent owners. Dickinson also claimed that women could never be successful inventors. Intrigued, Ida Tarbell decided to investigate further. She travelled to the Patent Office in Washington, D.C, and met with the head of the department (R.C McGill). McGill had compiled a list of women inventors, and the number was staggering at nearly two thousand – much more than Dickinson had said!

Tarbell wrote the following in her article: '*Three things worth knowing and believing: that women have invented a large number of useful articles; that these patents are not confined to 'clothes and kitchen' devices as the skeptical masculine mind avers; that invention is a field in which women has large possibilities.*'

In April 1887, Ida followed up her article with a showcase on women in journalism. She filled it with history, journalism practises, and advice. Tarbell included that journalism was an open field for women, but also adding that they should avoid crying so as not to appear weak. She gave other advice, trying to prepare any future female journalists about the job, and what it entailed.

In 1890, Ida Tarbell eventually had a falling out with Theodore Flood. The exact reasons behind her falling out with Flood are unknown, though there are some theories. He had placed his nineteen-year-old son's name on the Masthead above Ida Tarbell's, which was infuriating. She had been a dedicated worker, and had been in her thirties. To have a younger less-skilled person take that first name was an insult. She knew that it was either because he was male, or because the young man was related to Flood. Tarbell didn't want to be a 'hired gal', instead deciding to work for herself. This had always been her father's philosophy, and it served her well.

Something happened between Flood, and Ida. It was a secret that she would never reveal throughout her lifetime, but it was strongly believed that it was something sexual in nature. Whatever happened was enough to have her cut ties with *The Chautauqua*, and with Theodore Flood for the remainder of her career.

He had berated her, telling Tarbell that she was worthless, and had zero writing skills. Flood had tried to bring her down, after she had decided to leave the publication. But surprisingly, Flood wrote her a letter of recommendation, saying that *'Ida was a high-minded, honourable Christian woman whose strength and force of character I have learned to admire.'*

Ida Tarbell refused to say what had happened between them. She referred to it as *'The Meadville incident'*, or *'the affair'*. Ida feared Flood's influence greatly, no matter where she would end up. Tarbell said that *'she had disagreeable feelings about that episode'*. In a letter home, she wrote: *'What astonishes me, is that the Lord evidently means to let me have a chance in spite of the doctor.'*

Ida told her family to *'not let Flood worry you into any kind of retaliation'*. She was mainly worried about her brother, Will, fearing he would try and take his revenge against Flood. The year after she left the magazine, Flood ran for the U.S House of Representatives. Tarbell wrote to her parents, warning that *'Will must be careful not to let the personal side get a start. He at least must stay out of that for my sake, but on the grounds of decency and honesty, etc., Will surely can have all the material he'll have time to use. Work quietly, but keep it up.'*

Tarbell was still bitter about the whole incident between her and Flood. She said *'I don't care if he does go to Congress. He'll break his neck as sure as there are moral laws governing things, sooner or later, and he might as well do it in Congress as anywhere. He is one of those men who don't need to be helped do destruction. He's bound to kill himself unless, indeed, he sees the evil of his ways.'* Flood lost the congressional election, and lived until his mid-seventies. He died in 1915.

IDA TARBELL MOVES TO PARIS, FRANCE

Tarbell decided that she needed to put some space between her and Flood. She decided that it would be good for her to leave the United States for awhile. Paris, France, had always been the city of her dreams. She had always loved French history, and while she had been still employed at the *Chautauqua*, Tarbell had done some research for an article about Madame Roland (titled 'The Queen of the Gironde'). There were certain French historical figures which Tarbell greatly admired, such as Madame Roland, and Germaine de Stael. She was inspired by these women, and wanted to use them as subject matter for her writing.

On August 6, 1891, Tarbell travelled across the Atlantic from New York, to Paris, to new adventures. She almost didn't make the trip. Tarbell had arrived in New York hours before the ship was set to launch, but accidently went on the wrong ferry. She ended up two miles from her intended destination, at Jersey City. Tarbell had to fight to find transportation to make it to her ship on time. The pier was full, with thousands of passengers, and family to see them off.

Tarbell found the whole trip quite interesting. She was staying in the tourist class. She was interested in the other passengers. Ever the people watcher, she loved to study how people from different classes and backgrounds acted in the overcrowded quarters. People in the lower decks spoke multiple languages, unable to afford the higher-class tickets. The lower-class passengers stayed in the cramped steerage part of the ship. The passengers were close-knit, many of them friends or family members, and they entertained themselves with stories, dancing, and music.

She spent some time in Antwerp, before boarding a boat for Paris. Tarbell wanted to experience everything available to her. She was fascinated with the art museum, the full orchestra, and the art scene. Tarbell rode a merry-go-round, something she thoroughly enjoyed. There were all sorts of food, and games to enjoy – and she tried out the waffles, jumbles, hot candy, different cakes, and pegged balls at the small rag figures.

Throughout her journey, Tarbell wrote home to her parents and siblings, explaining to them everything she had experienced so far. She tried to put aside thoughts of her former job, and boss. Things had ended poorly, but she was determined to move on. Paris would be a new start, and a way for her to work on her dream project. She had saved hardly any money, and didn't plan on too many party nights in the city. Her goal, was to research as much as she could about Madame Roland.

By the time she arrived in Paris, Tarbell only had $150 to her name. She was used to living off a budget – as Tarbell had only ever earned a maximum of $100 monthly when she worked at *The Chautauquan*. It would be a challenge, but she was determined to succeed.

Her first order of business, was to find accommodations. Tarbell managed to convince three of her friends from *The Chautauquan* to rent an apartment with her. Before leaving for Paris, Tarbell had done some research, trying to determine where would be the best place to rent. She had decided that the Left Quarter, on the left bank of the Seine, would be a good area. Rent was cheap, as they were near the University campus. She thought it would be interesting to look for a place near the Museé de Cluny, because she liked the sound of it.

Josephine Henderson, was from Titusville. She had also attended Allegheny College, before working at the *Chautauquan*. Tarbell described Josephine as '*a handsome woman with a humourous look on life – healthy for me. I have never had a friend who judged my balloons more shrewdly or pricked them so painlessly.*' The second girl, was Mary

Henry. She had also worked at the *Chautauquan*, and had been from Silver Lake, New York. She had been raised by a militant household, of the Women's Christian Temperance Union Leader. The third roommate, was Annie Towle. She was from Evanston, Illinois, and was a friend of Mary Henry. Towle had moved to Paris on a whim.

Rent was expensive in Paris, and the four girls set off to look for a place. Some of the apartments were in poor condition. There were apartments with weird smells, or stains, and another with an insect infestation. It was disheartening, as the girls' budget was slim.

But they were finally able to find a decent second-floor apartment on Rue du Sommerard. It was a perfect location, being just a few blocks from Notre-Dame de Paris, the Sorbonne, and the Pantheon, as well as other beautiful locations. The newly-built Eiffel Tower (which had only been completed in 1889) was a novelty.

The girls were hoping to stay in Paris for two years. The apartment was unfurnished, and cost them $15 monthly. It contained two bedrooms, kitchen, salon, closet, and hall.

Tarbell said the following about furnishing their apartment: '*A French room with its pretty ceiling and walls, its chimney-piece, always surrounded by a mirror, and its hardwood floor is not difficult to make look well with very little furniture. Your kitchen, too, is furnished entirely, save stew pans and the like.*'

The girls took a minimalist approach to their new apartment, and decided to save money by shopping at small second-hand shops in Paris. It allowed them to get creative while staying within their budget. They had purchased Turkish curtains for two francs per yard at the *Bon Marché*, as well as pillows, and such. Their 'couch', was actually four steamer trunks, and a thin mattress.

They were able to eat quite cheaply in the city, as there were a great many bouillon shops, bakeries, and patisseries in their neighbourhood. For two cents, the baker would even roast their meat. The girls hated cooking, and were glad to have such conveniences around them.

Tarbell and her friends were greatly into the art scene. They were fond of Degas, Van Gogh, Manet, and Monet. She also visited the Can-can at the Moulin Rouge, and enjoyed it. Tarbell was quite social while living in Paris. Her and her roommates set up a language salon, where English and French speakers could gather, and practise the opposite language in a friendly environment. They also took private lessons. Within a few months, the girls were able to speak quite fluently, and spoke almost entirely in French.

Their landlady, Madame Bonnet, hosted weekly dinners for her tenants. The Chautauquan girls were always in attendance, as well as tenants from other parts of the world. There were young Egyptian men, including Prince Said Toussoum (cousin to the Egyptian ruler), as well as Charles Downer Hazen (future French historian, and professor at Smith College). The girls were able to meet a great deal of interesting people in Paris.

Tarbell knew that she needed to create income as a freelance writer. She set about contacting multiple American newspapers. These included the *Pittsburgh Dispatch, the Chicago Tribune,* and the *Cincinnati Times-Star*. In her letters to different publications, Tarbell was quite open about her new living arrangements, and her roommate situation. One of the publications (Portland's *Sunday Oregonian*), published an article about Tarbell living in Paris. It was titled '*Four Girls in Paris/A Great Co-operative Success/The Experience of Young Lady Students in Housekeeping in the French Metropolis*'.

Tarbell's first short story, '*France Adorée*', was published in the December 1891 edition of *Scribner's Magazine*. Her perseverance paid off, and Tarbell was able to gain a tutorship. Her freelance work enabled her to pay rent, and bills, but Tarbell's main goal during her stay in Paris, was to write a biography about Madame Roland, the leader of an influential salon during the French Revolution.

Ida Tarbell was greatly interested in writing about women, particularly about those that had helped shape history, but had become obscure historical figures. While researching Roland, she encountered Leon Marillier – one of Roland's descendants. It was a fortunate meeting, as Marillier gave Tarbell access to Roland's letters, and family documents. Tarbell was also invited to visit the Roland Country estate (*Le Clos*).

While staying in Paris, Tarbell took some classes at the Sorbonne. It was a much different experience than classes at Allegheny College. Sorbonne was much more laidback, and the professors would often not announce when their lectures were. They would show up out of the blue, and begin the lecture without a large introduction, skipping the regular formalities.

Tarbell's French was somewhat limited, but she was still able to understand much of her lessons. She would listen to lectures on politics, period painting, French revolutionary history, and 18th century literature. She was greatly interested in these classes, as they would help with her biography research. Tarbell studied the investigative and research techniques used by French historians while in Paris. The French used a compelling, concise style when presenting their evidence, and Tarbell followed suite. This specific French writing style aided her greatly, as she developed her skills as a narrative non-fiction author.

Tarbell had been greatly invested in her Roland research project, as she greatly admired the woman. But as her research continued, she started to become disillusioned. Tarbell had admired the woman for being an independent thinker, but she soon determined that Roland had been following her husband's lead. Roland had also been complicit in violence during the French revolution, which Tarbell determined had led to Roland's execution.

"This woman had been one of the steadiest influences to violence, willing, even eager, to use this terrible revolutionary force, so bewildering and terrifying to me, to accomplish her ends, childishly believing herself and her friends strong enough to control it when they needed it no longer. The heaviest blow to my self-confidence so far was my loss of faith in revolution

as a divine weapon. Not since I discovered the world not to have been made in six days . . . had I been so intellectually and spiritually upset.'
While Tarbell had been studiously delving into Roland's life in Europe, things at home were not going so well. Tarbell soon got the news that her father's business partner had committed suicide. Franklin Tarbell's business suffered greatly, and he found himself in a lot of debt. It was disconcerting news, especially since she was so far away, and didn't have enough resources to send money home to her parents.

Then in July 1892, she read in the newspaper that her hometown, Titusville, had been destroyed by both flood and fire. Oil Creek had flooded, and the inflammable material on the water had caught fire, and exploded. There had been more than 150 casualties. 72 Titusville residents were killed, along with 57 from Oil City. The floodwaters in Titusville had knocked over a benzene tank, which had caught fire. The fire had been almost a half-mile wide, easily burning down the wooden houses and businesses. Main Street had been particularly affected – with collapsed buildings from the highway to the creek. As the Tarbell family home was located on Main Street, this news was especially disturbing and saddening to Ida Tarbell – especially since she didn't know if her parents and siblings were even alive. Thankfully, she soon received a cablegram containing a single word: 'SAFE'. Tarbell soon discovered that her family, and the home had survived.

She had no money to send them, as she was on a very small budget already. She continued to write letters home, relieved that her family had been spared. Tarbell was worried about her father, as she had been following the Standard Oil Company, and Rockefeller, in recent times. The businessman had been going after independent contractors, and continually using persuasion and predatory practises all over the country. She knew that it would affect her and her brother's work, and worried about them relentlessly. Tarbell was worried especially about her brother's three young children – Scott, Esther, and Clara. She loved her nieces and nephew, writing to them often. For Christmas, she went out and found a small Parisian toy dog, and sent it to them.

Tarbell had been suffering some health issues, as well as needing to supplement her income. She had to take up more freelance jobs, as well as tutoring French people to learn English as a side job, trying to make ends meet. Despite this, she was struggling with food and clothing costs. She became ill off Parisian water, and experienced flu-like symptoms from the change in climate. Her mouth and gums ached, after not having proper dental care during her stay in Paris.

And then, in May 1892, her three roommates decided to move out. They had always been short-term, so it wasn't really a surprise to Ida Tarbell, but it was certainly a disappointment. She could no longer afford the high rent cost, and ended up moving to a much small place, at 17 Rue Malebranche.

There was another reason why Tarbell's budget had to be low – travel costs. Though her neighbourhood was mainly self-contained with school, and local stores nearby, Tarbell made sure to spend time exploring parts of France while living there. She reasoned that in order to properly write about France, and Madame Roland, she would need to experience all sorts of locations in France, and not just her neighbourhood.

During her first year in Paris, Tarbell spent a small amount of her budget on travel – and every Saturday, she and her roommates had taken trains, or boats to different locations such as Versailles. They visited small towns such as Beauvais, Chartres, Rheims, Pierrefonds, and Compiegne. On days with poor weather, they stayed closer to home, taking in the museums, and churches, walking about the city and familiarizing themselves with its beautiful architecture.

During her stay in Paris, Tarbell had managed to have multiple stories published. She had been sending out essays and stories since September, 1891, to publications such as the *Chicago Tribune, Omaha Bee, Cincinnati Times-Star, Boston Globe,* and the *Buffalo Express.*

Despite actually selling a few stories, Tarbell was still struggling to get by. This was because the stories only sold for an average of five dollars if they got accepted. And it could take months for her to receive the cheque in the mail. The published version was often quite different from her original work – as editors would pick over it, being choosy about what to publish. And there were layout changes, and often illustrations added. Tarbell often found it frustrating.

But then, with a stroke of luck, one of her short stories were published in *Scribner's Magazine* – which netted Tarbell a hundred dollars. Scribner's was still quite new, but it was considered one of the most prestigious publications for both fiction, and non-fiction, and Tarbell was incredibly excited to have her work published by them.

She had not planned on writing fiction, as it was neither her forte, nor was it her special interest. But Tarbell had decided to send off the short story regardless. Her story had been inspired by a French couple she'd tutored while in Titusville. She had referred to the man as Monsieur Claude, but never mentioned the wife's name. She borrowed certain elements from her real-life encounter with the couple, such as the bell being made from the French cannon. In other parts, Tarbell had fictionalized it – enough, she believed, that *'there is nothing in it which would give offence to Claude himself, I think, if he could read it'*.

As she continued to write about Paris, her readers became quite fascinated in the way that she portrayed the city, and its people. There had been a great deal of other American journalists in the past, many of whom had focused on the wealthy elite, and royalty. But with Tarbell, she could easily write about Paris' regular middle and lower class residents, while still making the readers quite interested.

While Americans often carried the notion that the poor had the intense pressure and obligation to try and work their way to the top, this idea was not the way things were done in Paris. Tarbell was quick to realize that Parisians often treated even lowly jobs as admirable, and that workers would be considered with respect because of the person's dedication. A person in poverty might not rise their way to the elite, but that was perfectly okay. It was perfectly fine if one did not advance among the ranks, as most would never have that opportunity. She found that the workers were not restless or envious in their line of work, which was a stark difference to the constant capitalistic rat race in the United States.

Tarbell had published some articles with the syndicate run by Samuel McClure. The first one was titled '*Marrying Day in Paris*', and it was about weddings held in public view. But there was one article in particular that caught Samuel McClure's eye. It was called '*The Paving of the Streets of Paris by Monsieur Alphand*'. The article described how the French would carry out large public works. McClure was greatly impressed with her writing style, and insisted to his partner, John S. Philips, that Tarbell should write for *McClure's Magazine*.

'*This girl can write*,' McClure had said, about Tarbell's article. '*I want to get her to do some work for the magazine.*'

McClure's was a new publication, that they had been trying to publish for the regular middle-class reader. Samuel McClure was so enthused by her work, that he personally travelled to Tarbell's apartment in Paris during a scheduled visit to France, and he asked if she could be the editor for his new magazine.

Tarbell described McClure as a '*will-of-the-wisp*'. He had stayed so long at the apartment talking to her, that he ended up missing his train. He was supposed to only be there for twenty minutes, but ended up visiting for more than three hours. McClure asked to borrow $40 from her, so that he could travel to Geneva, Switzerland. The $40 had been set aside for her vacation, and when she gave it to him, Tarbell assumed that she would never receive the money again. Surprisingly, his office wired her the money the very next day.

He was perfectly fine with hiring a woman for the magazine. McClure believed in inquisitive minds, no matter the gender, and spoke to

Tarbell with a deep sense of confidence, and enthusiasm about the project.

At first, Tarbell turned down the editor position. She wanted to stay focused on her Roland biography. She did, however, start to write for the magazine as a freelancer. This gave her freedom to continue working on her side projects. Tarbell's articles were about Parisian women – scientists, writers, and intellectuals. Though she didn't accept his proposal straight away, she and McClure quickly became friends, and she started to write commissioned pieces for him. This helped her financial situation a great deal, and allowed her the freedom to focus her attention on her writing again. He asked her to edit a series of articles about French morality in relation to America. Tarbell was also asked to translate French articles into English for the syndicate (which McClure would pay extra for), as well as seeking out new writers as the syndicate's Parisian editorial representative.

Through her new employment, Tarbell became acquainted with August Jaccaci (art director for McClure's). He often travelled to Paris on business, and when he stopped by Tarbell's apartment, he showed her the first issue of the magazine. Jaccaci was a perfectionist, who demanded that every detail be exactly as he'd planned it. There were times when he'd get angry with Tarbell, for failing to meet his professional standards. Jaccaci had been known to roar down the office corridor, with a fearful rage. Tarbell found him interesting to work with, impressed with the man's worldliness (as Jaccaci was a resident of both London, and Constantinople).

Because Tarbell had started to work with both Jaccaci, and McClure, she was able to expand her Paris orbit, to include a great deal more subjects, as well as sources. She was able to continually build up her confidence as a journalist, working on both her interviewing skills, and her research skills.

In 1893, Tarbell interviewed Louis Pasteur (French chemist, and microbiologist who worked on vaccinations, pasteurization, and microbial fermentation, and is considered the 'father of bacteriology'). She was fortunate to be able to go through his family photographs for the magazine. She visited him a second time, to write an article about his views on the future. The article sparked a regular section in the magazine, titled '*The Edge of the Future*'.

Tarbell got to interview other famous people for the '*Edge of the Future*'. This included Emile Zola (French novelist who had written a twenty-volume '*Les Rougon-Macquart cycle*', about a family under the reign of Napoleon III, as well as '*L'Assommoir*', and other works), Alphonse Daudet (French novelist who wrote '*Les Femmes d'Artistes*', '*Les Rois en Exil*', '*Sapho*', and '*La Belle Nivernaise*'). She also interviewed Alexandre Dumas (French novelist who wrote '*The Count of Monte Cristo*', '*The Three Musketeers*', as well as a great deal of magazine articles, and plays).

Despite working on the *McClure's* articles, Tarbell still set some time aside to continue writing the biography of Madame Roland. It was interesting to her, how little the city had changed since Roland had died. Tarbell often walked to the National Library, and she was able to walk through the neighbourhood where Roland's father had worked as a blacksmith. She could visit the location of Roland's church where she'd gotten her communion, the house where she'd been born, and also the prison where Roland had spent her last days. Tarbell could even walk along the exact same route that Roland had taken, as she'd been sent to the guillotine.

What truly aided Ida Tarbell in understanding Roland's life, was being able to read the plentiful letters that Roland had written. She could get a glimpse into the woman's mind, see how she had experienced life. She was a woman that had been surrounded by the Revolution, and she had been sucked in, becoming one of the most important individuals in the French Revolution.

Tarbell was offered the position of youth editor, which would replace Frances Hodgson Burnett. As soon as she had completed her biography of Madame Roland, Tarbell returned to United States during the summer of 1894. Her manuscript was still unpublished, but after gaining access to the unpublished letters and family documents, Tarbell was able to get a much clearer image of who Roland had truly been. Her Roland biography was soon published, and her detailed research into the woman's life was welcomed by readers, as it was a comprehensive and thoughtfully written biography.

TARBELL'S NAPOLEON BIOGRAPHY

In the summer of 1894, Ida Tarbell travelled by ship from Boulogne, to New York City. Her first stop, would be Titusville, Pennsylvania. It had been three years since she had seen her parents, siblings, nieces, and nephew. She was terribly excited to return home, even if it was just a short visit.

Before she had left Paris, Tarbell had asked her nieces what they would like as a souvenir. Clara asked for a French doll that could walk, and talk. Tarbell was determined to give her niece the requested present, though it turned out to be a much more expensive dll that she had planned for. In fact, she had spent so much on Clara's gift, that Tarbell almost couldn't afford the trip home.

It was a relief, and an extreme joy to return home. She was glad to see them alive and well, uninjured from the catastrophe that had taken so many Titusville lives while she'd been living abroad. Ida was extremely glad to be with her family again.

But after a few days, Ida Tarbell began to realize that her family was on the brink of despair. As she had already learned, Franklin Tarbell's business partner had committed suicide, and he had had to take on debt. Tarbell learned that they'd had to take out a mortgage on the family home. The economy was in a depression, leaving many people jobless, loans defaulted, people being evicted, and banks shutting down all around them. People were frightened that they wouldn't be able to provide for their families, and angry at their circumstances.

Franklin was having a difficult time running his oil barrel business, and Esther had had to return to teaching after a thirty-year hiatus, just so they could put food on the table. Will Tarbell had taken up a job as secretary-treasurer of the Pure Oil Company. It was a vertically integrated cooperative of drillers, transporters, refiners, wholesalers, and retailers who were fiercely resistant to Rockefeller. They were a rarity, one of the only long-term competitors against the Standard Oil Company.

Ida was greatly interested in the oil industry, and everything that her father and brother had been through since her departure. She had been receiving letters regularly from her family, and Will had been informing her about everything that had been going on. While she listened to her family discuss the oil industry, she recalled the unfinished manuscript Ida had been working on, while still employed at the *Chautauquan*. She thought a great deal about taking up that unfinished manuscript again, hoping to shed some light on the oil industry. This became especially true, when Will took her to the Pithole. It was nowhere near what she had imagined it'd be like, after spending so much time away. The area was devastated, with only stripped mines, and empty fields where the town used to be. Her and Will walked around all day, trying to find the exact location of their former house, her father's shop, the wells – everything that she had known in her childhood. It was a very surreal experience, strange and unsettling.

It was also strange to be home in Titusville again, surrounded by family and friends. Where she had worked on her career, and focused on becoming a better writer and journalist, many of her female friends from back home had gotten married and had children. Marriage and children, and running a household, were things that Ida didn't want for herself. She was a spinster, and was becoming comfortable with that label, as she was still desperately wanting to stay single and continue writing.

Her visit to Titusville was brief, and informative. It was good to reconnect with her family after so long, and important to hear what had been going on with their lives. Ida Tarbell was ready to move to New York City.

She was already quite familiar with living in a city, after being in Paris for a few years. New York had begun putting in taller buildings in Manhattan, as a great deal of companies needed the extra office space. Four years before Tarbell moved to New York, Joseph Pulitzer, for example, had built the World Building – which was the tallest skyscraper in the world at that time, at 309 feet high. New York had limited space, and needed to 'build up' – hence all the skyscrapers.

She started to work at McClure's, earning a yearly salary of $3,000. She worked at 743 Broadway, on the third floor. Parts of the city was becoming quite modernized. Clean, safe electricity with incandescent lighting had been installed in the business district, and there were elevated trains set up around the city to help with the high traffic flow. And telephones were becoming quite normalized, being installed in homes, and offices. This aided Ida and other journalists to communicate better, and faster.

Ida Tarbell rented an apartment at 1519 Eighteenth Street. Then, she later moved to 40 West Ninth Street. This time, she lived alone, instead of with roommates. She later moved again, to a much quieter neighbourhood near Gramercy Park. Tarbell lived at 120 East Nineteenth Street, where she stayed on for the rest of her life. There, she was able to properly focus on her work, instead of becoming distracted by the loud city life outside her window.

Ida Tarbell desperately wanted things to work, but she sometimes struggled at her job when it came to working with McClure. He was a big man, with a lot of ideas. People said that McClure had about three hundred ideas per minute, and that his right-hand man, John S. Phillips, was the only man around who knew which one was not crazy. Tarbell was glad that she would be paid a decent amount at her new job, and that she would have her name prominently displayed on her work. It was a daunting new job, though. McClure had decided against the regular practise of hiring on poorly paid freelance journalists to keep the magazine afloat. Instead, he hired full-time employees like Tarbell. He believed that by hiring people full-time, they'd produce better work, keeping their articles accurate, and entertaining – enough to entice readers to stick around.

A great deal of Tarbell's new coworkers greatly disliked her from the very start. Mostly, this was because she was relatively unknown in the New York publishing world, and also because she was a woman. There were also coworkers starting rumours that she and McClure were having a secret affair. They were both around the same age, and Tarbell was single. And many people knew that McClure was polyamorous, and often had extramarital affairs. To her coworkers, it seemed plausible, that that was why Ida Tarbell had been hired on at the magazine.

In 1895, McClure started to push Tarbell into larger writing assignments, and not just the regular small articles needed for the magazine. He believed that she would be the perfect person for these assignments, because of her relentless attention to detail, her never-ending curiosity, and her excellent research skills. McClure commissioned her to write a biography series on Napoleon Bonaparte. He had heard that his rival, the *Century Magazine*, were doing a series of articles on Bonaparte. People were fascinated with the deposed French ruler, and wanted to know more about him.

Tarbell accepted the Bonaparte assignment. She had already found Napoleon Bonaparte an interesting subject while living in Paris, and was more than happy to start writing about him. She said the following about it: *'I had been talking largely about devoting myself to French revolutionary history. If this wasn't that, what was? Napoleon, had pulled France out of the slough where she lay when Madame Roland had lost her head. I had a terrific need of seeing the thing through, France on her feet. Napoleon had for a time set her there, and brought back decency, order, and common sense.'*

Tarbell went to stay at Twin Oaks, in Washington, D.C., a seventeen-acre property in the Cleveland Park neighbourhood. It was home of Gardiner Green Hubbard (founder of the *National Geographic Society*, president of the *Bell Telephone Company*, and advocate for oral speech education for the deaf. His daughter, Mabel Gardiner Hubbard, married Alexander Graham Bell).

Hubbard had amassed a huge collection of documents and memorabilia pertaining to Napoleon Bonaparte. Tarbell also frequented the Library of Congress, and used resources from the U. S State Department. She was under an extremely tight schedule, as her first article was set to publish six weeks after she had first begun researching. Tarbell had referred to it as '*biography on a gallop*'.

Working on the Bonaparte series became quite useful for Tarbell, and she would later consider it a training ground for future work. She was able to perfect her style, and methodology for biographies. Tarbell was a big believer in the '*Great Man Theory*', and believed that remarkable individuals could shape society, just as much as society had shaped them. Tarbell's research, would be defined as '*historical investigative reporting*', as she would rely on the original documents, instead of believing secondary sources for her research.

Eventually, Tarbell moved out of Twin Oaks, fearing that she would be a burden on the Hubbard family. She moved into a rooming house on 1 Street Northwest, between Ninth and Tenth. The location enabled her to walk to the many government buildings, and continue her research into Bonaparte. Trying to meet McClure's deadlines, Tarbell pushed herself to finish the research, working for weeks non-stop.

She encountered historian Herbert B. Adams, from Johns Hopkins University, while working on the project. He taught at Smith College as well, and was an advocate for women's education. Adams believed in '*the objective interpretation of primary sources*', and Tarbell became influenced by this. This would become her method, while writing about her subjects.

When the Bonaparte articles were released, readers were quite fond of them. The articles doubled *McClure's* circulation to over 100,000 – and by the time the seventh and final Bonaparte article was published, the magazine had quadrupled their readership.

The *Century's* Bonaparte article was published in November 1894 (the same time as Tarbell's first installment into Bonaparte's life), though it didn't have nearly as much reader interest as Tarbell's articles. Her twenty-four-page article focused on the first twenty-six years of his life. Tarbell was quite pleased with the end result, especially as her article included the Hubbard engravings, and the published explanation from the collector, detailing how and why he had managed to collect more than 300 Napoleon treasures (the earliest dating back to 1791).

Tarbell gained a solid reputation as writer from this series, which helped her writing career immensely. The articles were then collected, and published in a book form. It was a success, earning Tarbell substantial book royalties for the remainder of her life. There were more than 70,000 copies printed of the first edition. Tarbell was pleased, stating that her work on Bonaparte *'turned her plans topsy-turvy'.* The book's popularity meant that Scribner's book publisher wanted to publish her book on Madame Roland.

TARBELL'S LINCOLN BIOGRAPHY

She also tackled a massive twenty-part biography series on Abraham Lincoln, titled '*The Life of Abraham Lincoln*'. She had been initially hesitant to work on the project, as she was nearly forty years old, and had yet to complete her Roland biography. Tarbell voiced her opinions on the matter, stating that '*If you once get into American history, I told myself, you know well enough that will finish France.*'

She had been fascinated with Lincoln since she had been very young. Tarbell could still recall the day that her parents heard the news about the President's assassination. Her father had come home from his shop, and her mother '*buried her face in her apron, running into her room sobbing as if her heart would break.*'

The Lincoln series was for *McClure's*, where she would be once again pitted against the *Century Magazine* series. For the rest of 1895, Tarbell split her time working on the Roland biography, as well as researching Lincoln. Tarbell went to John Nicolay, and spoke to him about the project. Nicolay told her that '*he and Hay had written all that was worth telling of Lincoln*'.

With that in mind, Tarbell decided she would start at Lincoln's early years. Abraham Lincoln had only been dead for thirty years by the time Tarbell started on her biography. Most people thought that there wasn't much that could be learned about the dead president, and thought her work would be fruitless.

She started to travel around the country, interviewing people who had known Lincoln, which included the man's son, Robert Todd Lincoln. He had shown his Lincoln papers to the *Century*, when they'd done a Lincoln series in 1890. Todd had claimed that he'd be making those documents unavailable again, until 26 years after his own death. Robert

Todd Lincoln showed Tarbell an early and never published daguerreotype of his father when he'd been younger.

It was winter when Tarbell travelled around the country, hoping to scour courthouses, and newspapers for important unpublished work to help with her research. She had to work with unheated horse carriages, and unreliable train schedules to get around. Kentucky was freezing in February, and the hotels and boarding houses were unheated. Even under the blankets and quilts, Tarbell refused to take off her socks because of how cold it was.

Tarbell visited several states' archives, and started to find pertinent material in different courthouse records, newspapers, and county histories. She was surprised and interested to know that a lot of those details had not appeared in the Nicolay-Hay compendium, the ten-part Lincoln biography.

She travelled around the Midwest, and discovered statements by people who had known Lincoln, or his family members. A Kentucky physician named Christopher Columbus Graham, had told a friend in 1882 (when he was 98 years old), that he'd gone to the wedding of Lincoln's parents, Nancy and Thomas. Graham's friend had quickly secured a sworn affidavit, realizing the importance of the man's story.

Tarbell didn't want to just take the man at his word, and started to look into proving that the old man had attended the wedding. She found a second oral account from Graham, which had been recorded by a Louisiana historian. This had occurred just before Graham's death in 1884, when he'd been 100 years old. After some more research, she decided that his story was accurate.

Tarbell then tracked down Henry Clay Whitney, close friend of the late President who had later written a biography about the man. She was interested in his notes from Lincoln's lost 1856 speech. She also contacted other witnesses to confirm his notes. Whitney's version of Lincoln's speech was printed in McClure's, but has been disproved by historians since then.

Ida Tarbell travelled to Kentucky, and Illinois, hoping to find out more about Lincoln's childhood. During her trip, she managed to interview hundreds of people who had known Lincoln, and tracked down leads to confirm the sources. Tarbell sent out hundreds of letters asking for images of Lincoln. She was met with a staggering amount of replies – more than three hundred unpublished Lincoln letters, and speeches.

Tarbell used these previously unpublished documents, to bring a new perspective to Lincoln's life. Tarbell's advice for those writing a biography, was that '*the writer should start by wiping out of his mind all that he knows about the man, start as if you had never before heard of him. Everything then is fresh, new. Your mind, feeding on this fresh material, sees things in a new way.*'

She contacted John H. Finley, during a trip to Knox College. This was where Lincoln had had his famous debate with Stephen Douglas in 1858. Finley was very young, working as college President. In later years, he contributed to Tarbell's research on the Standard Oil Company, and would eventually become editor of the *New York Times*. At one point, Tarbell uncovered a rumour that Lincoln had appealed to Queen Victoria to not recognize the Confederacy. She travelled to Europe to determine if the rumour had any merit. It turned out to be in vain, as it was a false rumour.

Her Lincoln series was published, and by December 1895, *McClure's* had had a substantial jump in circulation to 250,000. It jumped to 300,000 over the next few years, beating out all rival publications. Samuel McClure used the extra money to buy a bindery, as well as a printing plant. Some of the editors at *Century's Magazine* were scornful of Ida Tarbell's successful writing career, saying '*They got a girl to write the Life of Lincoln.*'

McClure was greatly pleased with Tarbell's research into Lincoln's life. He described her as being 'the face and soul of the magazine'. The March 1898 publication showed a large photo of Ida Tarbell, with a caption stating '*no name is more familiar to readers of McClure's*

Magazine than that of Ida M. Tarbell.' He was bombarded with letters, with readers asking for more of Tarbell's work to be published regarding Lincoln's life. They were all intrigued by her thorough research, and dedication.

Tarbell decided that she was through with being an editor, and wanted to stick to only writing. With the articles being published into book form, Tarbell's reputation had grown as a dedicated writer, and leading authority on Lincoln's life. In all, she wrote five books about Lincoln, and travelled the lecture circuit to talk to audiences about the late President's life.

Her biography about Lincoln, was published in 1900. It was met with some criticism, as some historians were less than happy with her portrayal of him. Albert J. Beveridge, U.S Senator (who had also written a Lincoln biography), created the verb *'to Tarbellize'*. It meant that she was lifting up Lincoln, all the while sanitizing his faults. *'The dear girl's efforts to fumigate are pathetic,'* Beveridge said about her biography. Throughout her lifetime, she continued to write articles, editorials, and books about Lincoln. Millions of people associated her name with the late president.

One of the downsides of having such tight writing schedules, as well as travelling so much, was that Tarbell's health began to decline. One night in 1896, after nearly collapsing, Tarbell checked herself into the Clifton Springs Sanitarium, near Rochester, New York. She was given proper attention, including a great deal of bed rest to recover. Tarbell also was given the *'water cure'* as treatment. The 'water cure' is also known as hydrotherapy. It uses water for pain relief and treatment, with some versions using baths, or Jacuzzis, to stimulate blood circulation, and for massage purposes. Tarbell would frequent the sanitarium when needed, over the next thirty years.

She continued to write for McClure throughout the late 1890s. Tarbell wrote about the United States' expansion into imperialism throughout the Spanish-American War, as well as other large stories. Tarbell was supposed to interview Nelson A. Miles in 1898. He was the commanding general of the United States. Unfortunately, that was when the USS Maine battleship was blown up in the Havana Harbour. She still went, and was able to observe at the U.S Army Headquarters.

Theodore Roosevelt had begun organizing the '*Rough Riders*' – the 1st United States Volunteer Calvary. While Tarbell was observing, Tarbell noted that Roosevelt '*kept bursting into the Army Office like a boy on roller skates*'.

She wanted to return to her old life in Paris, but Tarbell had her hands full. '*Between Lincoln and the Spanish-American War, I realized that I was taking on a citizenship I had practically resigned.*' In 1899, she moved to New York, and started to work as a Desk Editor for *McClure's*. Tarbell's income went from $3000 to $5000, and she was also given shares in the company, making her a part owner.

Tarbell rented an apartment in Greenwich Village, choosing the area because it reminded her of Paris. While in New York, Tarbell frequented the Hotel Brevoort, a place where Mark Twain had dined before.

Tarbell's plan had been to only work as editor while Samuel McClure was away for a few months. She quickly became known as an anchor in the office, as *McClure's* hired on a great deal of investigative authors. Stephen Crane was sent to Cuba during the war. Ray Stannard Baker was hired by the magazine to write about the Pullman Strike. Fiction editor, Viola Roseboro, worked diligently to bring authors into the magazine – discovering people such as O. Henry, Willa Cather, and Jack London. John Huston Finley, from Knox College, quit his job as president, in order to start working for *McClure's*.

STANDARD OIL COMPANY

During the early 20th century, McClure's had made a decision that they'd begin looking to *expose the ills of American society*. The publication had recently released a series of articles exposing crime in America, and they were eager to find their newest story. Tarbell and the other editors brainstormed what to work on next, eventually deciding on looking into growth of trusts. They considered looking into steel, and sugar. They eventually decided on oil.

Tarbell had had first-hand experience with the Pennsylvania oil fields in her youth, and so this aided in their decision. Also, the Standard Oil Company was owned by only one person – John D. Rockefeller. Believing that it would be easier to research the oil company if there was only one owner, Tarbell decided that that would be her newest project.

She travelled to Europe, to discuss the newest project with Samuel McClure. McClure had been off work for a few months, resting from exhaustion. However, when he heard Tarbell's idea, he was greatly enthused. Over the next few days, they discussed the idea at great length, while visiting a spa in Milan. McClure told Tarbell that she should follow the same biographical sketch format that she had used for Napoleon.

Tarbell travelled back to the United States, where she promptly handed over the Desk Editor job to Lincoln Steffens. Steffens was one of the leading muckraking investigative journalists, who had written articles about government corruption, and his leftist views. Ida Tarbell started to work with assistant John Siddall, looking into the oil industry's beginnings, Rockefeller's early interest, and the Standard Oil trust.

Franklin Tarbell confronted his daughter about the project, expressing his fears about her taking on Standard Oil. He feared Rockefeller's ruthlessness, fearing that he may go after her, and also the magazine.

Shortly after beginning the investigation, the magazine's financial status was threatened by one of Rockefeller's banks. Tarbell confronted the shocked bank executive, saying the following: '*Of course that makes no difference to me.*'

In the 1870s, John D. Rockefeller worked with his four business partners to create the Standard Oil Company. It had humble beginnings, and the company had a barrel-making shop, two refineries, railroad tank cars, docks on the lake, and land that had yet to be developed. Rockefeller was the company's largest share holder (with more than 10,000 shares), but was not the majority. He was the company's president. Other Rockefellers served as vice-president, directors, or stockholders.

The company grew over time, until it became a trust. They had corporate lawyers that would help the company by keeping up to date on the different state's laws. They even went ahead, and created a Standard Oil business in each state, as it would be easier to maintain these businesses through the top management structure.

It was believed that at first, Rockefeller and his associates weren't aware that they were committing unethical business practises. Following the Civil War, there wasn't a straightforward understanding of what fell under ethical, and unethical.

Rockefeller became greatly interested in absorbing the competition, or destroying the ones that stood in his way. This way, he could increase profit margins for every gallon of refined oil that he'd sell in the United States. Rockefeller got rid of the middlemen, shippers, wholesalers, purchasing agents – anyone that he could integrate into Standard Oil. The company was growing exponentially.

During this time, railroads would set their own prices for oil shipping, especially when their rail line was the only one being used in the area.

A lot of railroads were against the idea of having the government set a standard price for all railroads, because they preferred their own system.

Rockefeller refused to bow down when it came to the railroad executives. He wanted to have set prices, and reliable service. He made it so that he could get a shipping discount, as well as secretly negotiating rebates from the railroads for every barrel of oil that they shipped out. He also convinced railroad executives to give out private information about when their competitors would be shipping out their oil. Rockefeller's exchanged these private dealings and bargain rates, so that the railroads would have a reliable stream of deliverable goods, which meant they had a more reliable business.

Franklin Tarbell's business was negatively affected by the South Improvement Company scheme in 1872, that occurred between railroads, and the oil industry. In a four-month period, Standard Oil absorbed 22 out of 26 Cleveland competitors, which would later be referred to as 'The Cleveland Conquest', or 'The Cleveland Massacre'.

The biggest business coup occurring during the 'Cleveland Massacre', happened between Rockefeller, and Oliver H. Payne. He was the director of a Standard Oil refinery competitor, that was owned by Maurice and James Clark (these were Rockefeller's former partners). Rockefeller asked Payne if he wanted to sell the Walworth Run refinery, in exchange for teaming up with Standard Oil. He would receive stock shares in the deal.

Oliver H. Payne was the son of Henry B. Payne – an Ohio member of Congress. His mother's maiden name was Perry, and was a descendant of one of Cleveland's founding families. Payne was rich enough, and was not in the business to get out of poverty. He was, however, looking to help improve managing a promising enterprise. He agreed to Rockefeller's offer, and became another competitor to be one of his allies.

Rockefeller continued to talk with refinery owners, and offering them stock options instead of cash. John Stanley was one who took him up on the offer. They would hold onto their stocks until they were worth a great deal, and then sell them off for enough money to support themselves and their families. Another refinery that Rockefeller purchased, was from Hugh and John Huntington. The two brothers had different takes on accepting the offer. John took the stock option, while Hugh asked for cash. They had different results from this deal. Hugh never got rich. His brother became incredibly wealthy, enough to support Cleveland charities over the years.

Ida Tarbell became enraged by the Standard Oil Company's unfair tactics, especially with rumours that Rockefeller was a predatory businessman, preying on the weak, and threatening them into selling at lowered prices to line his own pockets. Tarbell wrote to the leaders about how she put her father, as well as other small oil companies out of businesses. The Standard Oil Company had been secretly working with the railroads, jacking up the prices on oil shipments for independent oil men. The company received discounts and rebates for their members, to offset the high rates – and thus, put them out of business. Standard Oil went from 1,500 barrels of oil per day, to 11,000.

After word got out about Rockefeller's secretive deals involving railroad shipping rates, there was a huge uproar. More than three thousand people protested against Standard Oil. Franklin Tarbell was actively involved in marches, and protests against the South Improvement Company, and tipped over Standard Oil railroad tankers.

Protesters met at the Titusville Opera House, and they held signs saying '*Down with the conspirators*', and other similar messages. They even created their own group, titled '*Petroleum Producers Union*'. They were determined to prevent any oil from getting into the hands of Standard Oil, or anyone associated with them.

Pennsylvania state legislators, and U.S congressmen, attended a hearing in Washington, D.C. They discussed Standard Oil's business practises.

During the testimony, they spoke of 'restraint of trade', 'antitrust', 'monopoly', and even 'unfair competition'. But though they discussed it at length, no action was taken against Rockefeller. Eventually, however, the government of Pennsylvania disbanded the South Improvement Company.

The day after the hearing, he travelled to the oil region. He was determined to show that he was unafraid. He was not very popular, as Rockefeller had a reputation as a harsh businessman, and in his personal life, he hated most things about the living in the oil region. He was considered extremely conservative, and hated drinking, or alcohol. Rockefeller was not a social man.

Although many people disliked Rockefeller, and the way he ran his business, he was still at the very top of the oil industry. Rockefeller had amassed a huge wealth, having created such a profitable business.

As with all her work, Ida Tarbell meticulously did all her research on her subject, using as many investigative reporter techniques as she could. She dove into private archives, looking into public documents throughout the country. She conducted oral interviews, proving that Standard Oil had used strong-arm tactics, and manipulated competitors, and railroad companies to reach their goals.

When writing, Ida Tarbell would spread out all her papers out on the desk. She liked her desk to be covered with all her research. When writing 'The History of Standard Oil', Tarbell would work from home in her study. She would only visit the McClure's office once a day, while taking a writing break.

Her New York home had a partners desk filled with stacks of paperwork, and a bentwood chair. She would collect all the transcripts, clippings, and books that she needed, and keep them close for when she needed to consult them. Tarbell would finish a chapter and hand it in, then go through all the material again – rearranging its order for her next article in the series. When she worked from her Twin Oaks property, Tarbell had a mahogany desk, which she used in her library.

One crucial piece of evidence – an 1873 book titled '*The Rise and Fall of the South Improvement Company*' – became incredibly important to her research. Standard Oil, having been complicit in many of South Improvement Company's illegal schemes, had tried to destroy every copy of the book. Tarbell tried in vain to find a copy, and was finally successful, after discovering that the New York Public Library still had a copy on hand. She was incredibly fortunate to have found the book.

Another important break in the story, was with an office boy working with the Standard Oil headquarters. The office boy had been instructed to destroy company records that detailed how the railroads were giving Standard Oil advance information about refiner's shipments. They were then able to undercut the refiners. The office boy had been destroying records, when he stumbled across a few documents that had his Sunday school teacher's name on them. The teacher was a refiner. He secretly took the papers to his teacher, and showed them to him. The teacher then brought the papers to Tarbell in 1904.

Having access to documents such as these, aided Tarbell's research a great deal. She needed to prove that the company was using shady, illegal practises to further their company. Documents such as these were proof that she could use for her exposé. It was the sort of smoking gun document that she had been after.

'*The History of the Standard Oil Company*', was an impressive piece of investigative journalism. Published in 1904, it was 815 pages long. Ida Tarbell spent ages doing painstaking research on the subject. The book created a great deal of change, that destroyed reputations, and changed public policy.

Robber barons, public men who had colluded to create powerful monopolies, were rampant in the beginning of the 20th century. By the time Theodore Roosevelt had become the President of the United States, there were a great deal of journalists who were intent on bringing illegal practises, underhanded deals, and the men responsible for such actions to the page. Exposing them and their actions, in hopes that they could create change.

One of America's most recognizable investigative journalists, Ida Tarbell, had decided to take on one of the most powerful businessmen in the country. Her dedication to her work, coupled with her intensely meticulous documentary skills aided her greatly in her task.

John Davison Rockefeller, had spent his whole life building an empire on black gold. He had risen to the top, becoming the richest person of the Gilded Age. He had incredible business skills, and was considered the guiding force for the Standard Oil Company, which was the country's *'most sprawling corporate trust'*. He was considered the most important figure in shaping America's oil industry, and played in important role in the country's industrial development, as well as the rise of the modern corporation. After the book was published, Rockefeller became the most hated American businessman, some envying his success, while others despising his ruthless actions in a position of power.

Tarbell was still working as a staff writer for *McClure's Magazine*. She started writing about Standard Oil, first introducing her work as a magazine series. This new form of journalism, was dubbed *'muckraking'*, a term that had been borrowed John Bunyan's 'Pilgrim's Progress', about a man with a muckrake, who would forever be cleaning all of the muck off the floor. Her new style of muckraking took on great traction, and soon, there were a great deal of journalists using her new method to uncover wrongdoings throughout the country.

Roosevelt said the following about muckrakers: *'The man who never does anything else, who never thinks or speaks or writes save of his feats with the muckrake, speedily becomes, not a help to society, not an incitement to good, but one of the most potent forces of evil'.*

Tarbell was not fond of the muckraker label, and she wrote about it in an article titled *'Muckraker or Historian'*. She explained why she had gone after the oil company, and said *'this classification of muckraker, which I did not like. All the radical element, and I numbered many friends among them, were begging me to join their movements. I soon found that most of them wanted attacks. They had little interest in balanced findings. Now I was convinced that in the long run the public they were trying to stir would weary of vituperation, that if you were to secure permanent results the mind must be convinced'.*

Through her relentless work, Tarbell had forever tarnished John D. Rockefeller's reputation. Her analysis had changed the public's perception forever, and it wasn't something he could easily shake off.

Rockefeller refused to ever discuss Tarbell's exposé in public. One of his employees said that Rockefeller had privately pulled them aside at one point, and said that '*much of what my own son knows about standard Oil, is his memory of what he has read in Tarbell's book, with only here and there a statement of fact by me*'.

Some of the techniques that Tarbell had used at the time, are still being used by investigative journalists today. She had managed to gather information about a highly secretive corporation, and its chief executive. She was persistent in her quest for the truth, using every resource she had possible – legal documents, government documents, as well as interviewing sources both inside and outside of the company.

Tarbell's book on Standard Oil Company was turned into a play in 1905, titled '*The Lion and the Mouse*'. Ida Tarbell was offered the lead role in the play, and a $2500 weekly salary for the twenty-week run. She declined the role. The play was a success, with 686 continuous performances. The play was a record-setter for an American play in New York, and four road companies also took the play on the road.

Samuel Clemens (Mark Twain), introduced Tarbell to Henry. H. Rogers – vice-president at Standard Oil, and who was considered to be the third man after John D. Rockefeller, and his brother, William Rockefeller. Rogers' career had begun in the Pennsylvania oil fields where Tarbell had been raised, during the American Civil War.

Rockefeller had bought out Rogers and his partner, but then later, Rogers ended up joining the trust.

In 1902, Tarbell interviewed Rogers several times at the Standard Oil's headquarters. Rogers was normally considered a very guarded man when it came to business and financial matters, but with Tarbell, he was incredibly forthcoming. It was believed that he may have been under the impression that her work on Standard Oil would be complimentary. Even after the first few articles were published in *McClure's*, Rogers continued to speak freely to Tarbell about the company.

From November 1902 to 1904, *McClure's* published nineteen articles about Standard Oil. The first article was published with pieces by both Ray Stannard Baker, and Lincoln Steffens. Their combined efforts became crucial in creating the newest form of investigative journalism, known as muckraking.

Author Steve Weinberg said the following, in his 2008 book '*Taking on the trust: the epic battle of Ida Tarbell and John D. Rockefeller*': '*Tarbell's biggest obstacle, however, was neither her gender nor Rockefeller's opposition. Rather, her biggest obstacle was the craft of journalism as practised at the turn of the twentieth century. She investigated Standard Oil and Rockefeller by using documents – hundreds of thousands of pagers scattered throughout the nation – and then amplified her findings through interviews with the corporation's executives and competitors, government regulators, and academic experts past and present. In other words, she proposed to practise what today is considered investigative reporting, which did not exist in 1900. Indeed, she invented a new form of journalism.*'

Author and historian Frank Luther Mott, was quoted as saying '*it was one of the greatest serials ever to appear in an American magazine*'. Tarbell's articles contributed to the dissolution of Standard Oil, as well as the formation of the Clayton Antitrust Act. Tarbell had also written a two-part character study on Rockefeller, which is considered one of the first CEO profiles ever published. She had never met or spoken with the man, as he was a very private man. Rockefeller referred to as Tarbell as '*Miss Tarbarrel*'.

One thing that Ida Tarbell was adamant about, was that her biography could not paint her subject as entirely 'good', or 'bad'. People were much more complex than that. When researching Rockefeller, Tarbell tried to keep a balance between good and evil, otherwise it would be 'a biographical sin'. Tarbell's perspective on Rockefeller was ruthless at times, but she made sure to include his accomplishments. Her last chapter, was titled '*The Legitimate Greatness of the Standard Oil Company*'.

Her previous biographies of Lincoln and Bonaparte were considered easier tasks. Those subjects were dead, and her research was based off of biographies already written, as well as documents and interviews from people who had once known them.

But with Rockefeller, the man was a powerful businessman who was still very much alive. Rockefeller objected greatly to a woman journalist digging into his business, and revealing everything to the public. There could be potential consequences if Tarbell wrote inaccurate information (as she could be accused of libel, or defamation of character). Rockefeller had a lot to lose if the book revealed too much.

One of Tarbell's greatest challenges, was the style of journalism that was used during the twentieth century. Tarbell ended up creating own style of journalism, called 'investigative journalism', as that sort of thing didn't exist in 1900. It is the same tactics that journalists still use to this day, hoping to have as much success as Tarbell's work.

Throughout her writing career, Ida Tarbell had written thousands of letters, multiple books including the exposé on the Standard Oil Company, as well as hundreds of articles for both magazines, and newspapers. She also spoke publicly around the country for decades. Though many of her private thoughts remained private, there had been a great deal of information to glean about the prominent woman journalist.

That could not be said about Rockefeller. He was an intensely private person, who kept his thoughts closed off from the public. He hardly ever made public appearances. Rockefeller wrote a memoir, titled '*Random Reminiscences of Men and Events*'. The book was an interesting glimpse into Rockefeller's private life, and it was also intended to defend himself against Tarbell's scathing journalism, hoping to regain his reputation to what it had once been. It did not have its intended effect, as his memoir was considered too brief, and didn't go into depth as much as readers and critics hoped.

Tarbell was not the first journalist to take on Standard Oil. In 1894, journalist Henry Demarest Lloyd investigated the oil company, and Rockefeller. Henry Demarest Lloyd was a political activist, and muckraking journalist. He worked for the *Chicago Tribune*, and his article against Rockefeller was published in the March 1881 issue of *the Atlantic* (titled '*The Story of a Great Monopoly*'). Over time, he expanded on the article, before publishing it in a book titled '*Wealth Against Commonwealth*'. His book did not receive nearly as much attention as Tarbell's, and this was because it contained a great deal of factual errors, and readers judged it to be too accusatory.

Tarbell's articles and book were well-received, and became a bestseller. Her work led to the Hepburn Act in 1906, to oversee the railroads. Also, the 1910 Mann-Elkins Act (giving the Interstate Commerce Commission power over oil rates), and the FTC (Federal Trade Commission) opening up in 1914.

AFTER THE STANDARD OIL COMPANY BOOK WAS PUBLISHED

Tarbell had written for McClure's from 1894-1906. But as time went on, Samuel McClure became less involved in his own publication, often being an absentee publisher. He would occasionally drop in to veto people's ideas, as well as Tarbell's orders.

Tarbell found this sort of workplace incredibly stressful, as McClure's behaviour was becoming erratic. Coupled with the stress of losing her father to gastric cancer the year before, Tarbell was struggling to maintain the publication to her standards.

Franklin and Esther Tarbell had travelled to Philadelphia to be visit their son. Franklin fell ill with stomach troubles, and became quite tired. He thought that it was just a stomach bug, or something minor. When he continued to be sick, Franklin was admitted to the Clifton Springs sanitarium in New York.

Franklin didn't get better with treatment, and the doctors told the family that he had gastric cancer, and would likely die. Franklin refused to die at the sanitarium, instead opting to return home with his family. Though he seemed to be getting better at first, his health took a nosedive. Franklin died on March 1st, 1905. He was seventy-five years old. He was buried at Woodlawn Cemetery, in Titusville, Pennsylvania.

In June 1906, Ida Tarbell, and John Phillips, decided to leave McClure's for good. They resigned, and soon after, Ray Stannard Baker, John Siddall, and Lincoln Steffens also left. Tarbell and Phillips pooled their money together, and created the Phillips Publishing company. They bought *The American Magazine* (which had previously been called *Leslie's Monthly Magazine*). Phillips was president of the company, while Tarbell worked as associate editor until 1915. They decided that instead of muckraking journalism and what was 'wrong' with society, their magazine would focus on what was 'right'.

In 1906, Tarbell purchased a forty-acre farm in Redding Ridge, Connecticut, and called the property 'Twin Oaks'. After purchasing the property, she had a few relatives come to live with her. Tarbell lived with her sister, Sarah, in Easton, Connecticut, at Rock House and Valley Roads. Her niece and nephew moved into a cottage on the property. Tarbell's brother, Will, moved to the Twin Oaks with his wife, after he suffered an emotional breakdown. Tarbell lived nearby other authors, including Mark Twain, and several people in the New York publishing world. She often had friends visit the farm.

Living on a large farm property was not always an easy task. The house and garden always required a great deal of work. Tarbell wrote the following about life at Twin Oaks: '*Things happened: the roof leaked; the grass must be cut if I was to have a comfortable sward to sit on; water in the house was imperative. And what I had not reckoned with came from all the corners of my land: incessant calls – fields calling to be rid of underbrush and weeds and turned to their proper work; a garden spot calling for a chance to show what it could do; apple trees begging to be trimmed and sprayed. I had bought an abandoned farm, and it cried loud to about its business.*'

Despite all the hard work she had to put into her property, Tarbell continued to write articles for *The American Magazine*. She did some investigating into tariffs, and how they would impact American businesses and consumers. At one point, she travelled to Chicago, and did some investigative work on their public transportation system. Tarbell met Jane Addams (social worker, woman's suffragist, and political activist), and in 1908, Tarbell stayed at Hull House. She involved herself with the many programs set up there, including job skills, homemaking skills, and classes teaching immigrant women English.

In 1911, Tarbell and the other editors decided that it was time to sell *The American Magazine* to *Crowell Publishing*. John Phillips held onto his remaining interests in the company for a few years, but eventually sold them to Crowell in 1915. Phillips stayed on as a consultant to the magazine, and John Siddell took up the editor position. Tarbell decided to go into freelance writing.

From 1912-16, Tarbell travelled the United States, as she worked on a series of article about the positive side of American businesses. She met with factory owners, as well as their families. She said the following about her muckraking reputation: '*Was it not the duty of those who were called muckrakers to rake up the good earth, as well as the noxious?*'

Tarbell soon became quite fascinated by Thomas Lynch, of the *Frick Coke Company*. Lynch had become insistent on providing his workers with decent living conditions, and was adamant that his business hold a '*Safety First*' approach, instead of allowing workers to become injured or maimed in workplace accidents.

Another company that caught Tarbell's interest, was Henry Ford's *Ford Motor Company*. He held strong beliefs that by paying his employees a decent amount of money, they would create excellent work. Instead of having three men assemble each vehicle by hand, Ford decided to upgrade his factories to include mass production and assembly lines, making everything run smoother and more efficiently.

Ida Tarbell was also a feminist. Author Steve Weinberg wrote that Ida Tarbell '*was a feminist by example, but not by ideology*'. Some Feminist scholars considered Tarbell an enigma, because although she embraced the movement, she also was a critic. There were times where Tarbell questioned and challenged the logic of women suffrage.

She had become exposed to the suffragette movement at a very young age, when her mother would have meetings at the family home. She had found herself put off by some of the women, like Mary Livermore and Frances Willard, who would completely ignore and shut Tarbell out of the meeting. It was with her father's friends that she felt more comfortable, as they included her in their business. The Suffragette movement did, however, influence Tarbell to attend college and get a decent education, which she put to great use.

From 1909, Tarbell had been writing about women, and their traditional roles. She felt a sense of alienation from the suffrage movement, referring to it as 'anti-male'. She believed that 'the drive for suffrage' was considered a 'misguided war on men'. Tarbell wrote about how women should embrace their home life, and their family. She believed that women *'had a true role as wives, mothers, and homemakers'*.

There were people in her life that had considered her an ally, that became distraught at the idea that Tarbell was speaking out against women's rights and the suffragist movement – especially since she was speaking to anti-suffragist organizations. In 1912, Tarbell published an article called *'Making a Man of Herself'*. Activists and readers were all greatly upset by her article.

Historian Robert Stinson believed that she may have been making a public statement about the sort of ambiguity that she'd lived with all her life. *'It defined women's roles based on their nature, and saw attempts to push the boundaries into men's realms as unnatural.'*

Emily McCully (author of the 2014 book *'Ida M. Tarbell: the woman who challenged big business - and won!'*) wrote the following: *'that suffrage was a human's rights issue seemed not to occur to her, perhaps because, as a historian, she was much better looking backward than she was at anticipating the future'.*

Tarbell created a collection of her essays on women, and published them in a book titled *'The Business of Being a Woman'*. It was not well received. It had tributes to early women supporters, like Susan B. Anthony, and Elizabeth Cady Stanton. Tarbell's mother, Esther Tarbell, had been a suffragette for her entire life. She heavily criticized her daughter's book, as well as her opinion on the suffragette movement, and women's rights.

'*That title was like a red rag to many of my militant friends*,' Tarbell said about her book. '*The idea that woman had a business assigned by nature and society, which was of more importance than public life disturbed them; even if it was so, they did not want it emphasized*.'

In 1920, when American women were allowed to vote, Tarbell's opinions shifted. She started to embrace the suffrage movement. In 1924, she wrote an article for *Good Housekeeping* trying to dispel the myth that suffrage had been a failure. '*Twenty million women did vote, and should vote*', wrote Tarbell about the suffrage movement.

When she was asked if a woman could ever be President of the United States, Tarbell said that women had been rulers in a great many nations throughout history. Elizabeth I of England, Catherine the Great of Russia, Catherine de' Medici of France, and Louise of Mecklenburg-Strelitz of Prussia were all strong examples of women leaders.

Tarbell revisited the idea of helping women workers who '*had no choice but to work, often under horrifying conditions*'. She focused her attention on workplace safety, particularly the factories where women worked.

Tarbell became a Taylorism advocate. It was a system designed for scientific management of production, which encouraged its use in home economics. Tarbell even became a member of the Taylor society. When working on an article titled '*The Golden Rule of Business*', Tarbell visited more than 55 business, to study how they mixed '*scientific management and Christian values*' to work together. Molding these two belief systems, Tarbell decided, was the best way to protect all the workers, as well as maximizing profits. Tarbell was the founding member of the Author's League in 1914. It was a collective to support working writers that later became the Authors Guild.

In 1915, Tarbell had a career shift, when John Siddall became editor for the *American Magazine*. She joined the Chautauqua Science and Literary Circuit, which was a lecture and entertainment tour frequented with singers, public speakers, and acts such as yodelers, and trained dogs. Tarbell trained with Frank Sargent of the American Academy of Dramatic Arts, to improve upon her public speaking skills. Being on tour like that was a brutal experience. Tarbell wrote about how exhausting it was. She had signed up for a seven-week circuit, and she visited a new location for each of the forty-nine days on tour. When the tour ended, Tarbell was utterly exhausted. Despite the fatigue, she signed on for another few years to tour the United States. During her lecture tours, Tarbell would discuss a great deal of subjects – everything from politics, trusts, labour, women in the workforce, tariffs, peace, and the evils of war.

WORLD WAR I

In April 1917, the United States joined the Great War. Ida Tarbell was contacted by President Woodrow Wilson, asking if she would like to join a new committee. It was called the 'Women's Committee of the Council of National Defense'. The Committee's goal, was to encourage women to take up specific roles during the Great War. These activities included knitting, sewing, running daycare centers while women started to work in factories, bandage making, etc. They were also tasked with planting vegetable gardens, food drying, and canning – all to combat the war-time food crisis.

At first, the Suffragette members on the committee were greatly displeased that Tarbell had been invited. It didn't take long, however, that Tarbell's warm spirit won over the Suffragette members. Tarbell worked with both the Men's council, and the Women's Committee – often working as a go-between.

1917 was a difficult year for Tarbell. In September, her mother died. It was a great loss, as she had already lost her father years before. The year after, on returning to Washington, D.C, Tarbell collapsed. She was brought to Johns Hopkins, and was diagnosed with tuberculosis. She spent three months in the hospital recovering. Unbeknownst to her, her doctor also diagnosed Tarbell with the early stages of Parkinson's disease. She only discovered her diagnosis a few years later, when her tremors started to get so bad, that it affected her handwriting.

The Women's Committee was disbanded in 1918, when WWI ended. Tarbell decided that she would return to Paris, France. She longed to return to the European city that she had enjoyed so much. Paris in the late 1890s, and Paris postwar were very different experiences.

She was able to reunite with some of her old *McClure's* magazine colleagues, as they were in the city for the Paris Peace Conference. John S. Phillips was working as editor of the Red Cross Magazine, and Ray Stannard Baker was assistant to President Woodrow Wilson.

President Wilson had hoped to have Tarbell work in the official U.S legation, but what Tarbell didn't know, was that Robert Lansing (Secretary of State) refused to have a female on his team.

Tarbell started to write for the Red Cross magazine, and she started to travel around Paris to interview them on how the Great War had affected them. She also travelled around the countryside, and interviewing farmers who were living in the wreckage of their war-torn country homes, now reduced to rubble.

After carefully detailing the Parisian wartime experiences, Tarbell decided to focus primarily on the female perspective. Her articles on the average French women, were titled '*The French Woman and her New World*', '*That Brave Northwest*', and '*The Homing Instinct of Woman*'. In later years, Tarbell's career focused on lecturing, writing, and her social work. She was still working the lecture circuit, while working as a freelancer journalist.

In 1919, Tarbell decided to change things up by changing from writing only non-fiction works, to trying her hand at fiction. Her first and only novel was titled '*The Rising of the Tide*'.

She went back to writing articles – this time about the disarmament conference for *McClure's*, which was later published in book form (titled '*Peacemakers – Blessed and Otherwise*').

Tarbell served on two Presidential Conferences. The first one, was President Wilson's Industrial Conference in 1919, and represented the Pen and Brush Club of Gramercy Park, New York City. She served on a committee that looked into hours of labour, along with Robert Brookings. Tarbell's committee had a great deal of recommendations for women workers, to improve upon their health and work culture. These recommendations included women workers working eight-hour days, six days a week, and not having any shifts between 10 PM to 6 AM. One of the representatives at the Conference, was John D. Rockefeller – the same man that Tarbell had written extensively about, in her Standard Oil Company exposé.

Tarbell's second Presidential Conference, was President Warren G. Harding's Unemployment Conference, in 1921. It had been suggested by Herbert Hoover, to address the recession. Tarbell worked on multiple communities in the conference, such as Public Works, Publications, Organization, Civic Emergency Measures, and Standing Committee of the Conference.

Tarbell decided to write a biography on Judge Elbert H. Gary (chairman of the U.S Steel Corporation). At first, Tarbell was extremely reluctant to write the biography. But Judge Gary convinced her that it would be a good idea. He hoped that if Tarbell was able to uncover any wrongdoings by his company, then Gary would be able to correct these errors, and do better.

When she published the Judge Gary biography, Tarbell earned $10,000 for her work. She personally believed that the book was a success, and she described it as being 'courageous work'. But critics were less than enthused. They accused Tarbell of writing a 'cowardly' biography. One review (titled '*The Taming of Ida Tarbell*'), accused her of falling in with her sworn enemy – big corporations and businesses.

During the 1920s, Tarbell decided to write a few articles about Benito Mussolini, for *McCall's magazine*. She portrayed Mussolini in a good light, considered flattering – even comparing him to Napoleon.

One of Tarbell's former colleagues, Viola Roseboro, met up with her in Italy. She said the following: '*I heard her let go about that dimple several times. All those things that are at such a variance with the old work horse she calls herself and to the serious worker she is and is known for pleases me a lot*'. Viola Roseboro speculated that Tarbell may have seen Mussolini as '*finishing the work of the Progressive Era at the small price of a few civil liberties*'.

The last business biography that Tarbell worked on, was about Owen D. Young (who was the president of General Electric, who had founded both NBC, and Radio Corporation of America). Speculations at the time, was that Owen Young was considering running for president, and thought that Tarbell's book would make a good campaign biography.

She was later approached by Arthur Schlesinger Sr., to contribute to his historical series in 1923. He was working on '*A History of American Life*'. It took years for Tarbell to complete the work, finishing '*The Nationalizing of Business*' in 1936.

During this time, Tarbell also stayed busy by serving as President of the Pen and Brush Club for decades. She also participated in both the Colony Club, and the Cosmopolitan Club. The Colony Club, was a female-only private social club, in New York City. It was for wealthy women, whose headquarters were located at 120 Madison Avenue (between East 30th and East 31st Street). The club was often the site of Suffrage rallies. The headquarters hosted a great deal of athletic programs, with tennis, squash, a swimming pool, and spa services.

The Cosmopolitan Club, was a private social club located at 122 East 66th Street. It was a woman-exclusive club that had esteemed members such as Eleanor Roosevelt, Pearl Buck, Margaret Mead, Abby Aldrich Rockefeller, and Jean Stafford.

TARBELL'S DEATH AND LEGACY

When Tarbell was 82 years old, she completed her autobiography. It was titled '*All in a Day's Work*'. The 1939 book garnered mixed reviews. She wrote extensively about her childhood days in the oil fields, her determination to her biography writing, her time in Paris, and a great deal more.

Tarbell was working on another book, titled '*Life After Eighty*', but it was never completed. She was admitted to the Bridgeport, Connecticut hospital in December 1943. By January 6, 1944, Ida Tarbell died of pneumonia. She had been 86 years old.

In 1993, Easton, Connecticut declared that the 'Ida Tarbell House' was a National Historic Landmark. The Ida Tarbell House, was 'Twin Oaks', located at 320 Valley Road, Easton. This was where she had lived from 1906 until her death. She had done the majority of her writing, in the first-floor study.

In 2000, Tarbell was posthumously inducted into the National Women's Hall of Fame, located in Seneca Falls, New York. On September 14, 2002, the United States Postal Service had a stamp created to honour Ida Tarbell's legacy. It was part of a four-stamp series, honouring multiple female historical journalists.

For years after her death, Ida Tarbell's life, and journalism skills have been studied at great length. In 1993, Everett E. Dennis, Executive Director of the Freedom Forum Media Studies Center, at Columbia University, declared that Ida Tarbell had helped create modern journalism, particularly investigative journalism.

Historian Doris Kearns Goodwin, author of '*The Bully Pulpit*', stated that Tarbell's Standard Oil series, was a '*landmark series that would affirm her reputation as the leading investigative journalist of her day*'.

Ellen F. Fitzpatrick, Historian and Professor of History at the University of New Hampshire, said that Tarbell was one of the greatest American journalists of the 2oth century.

Tarbell's work '*The History of the Standard Oil Company*', was listed as No. 5, in a 1999 list created by New York University. The list marked the top 100 works, from 20th century American journalism.

Daniel Yergin, historian and author of '*The Prize: The Epic Quest for Oil, Money, and Power*', stated that Tarbell's Standard Oil book was '*the single most influential book on business ever published in the United States*'.

Steve Weinberg (who had been the one-time executive director of the non-profit *Investigative Reporters and Editors, Inc.*), developed training programs based off Tarbell's investigative techniques. Historically, there had been muckrakers (or 'yellow journalists'), that would write stories that had little no factual evidence. They would focus instead on clickbaity and sensationalist headlines, in an effort to sell papers – instead of focusing on journalistic integrity.

But there were other journalists that were labeled muckrakers (such as Upton Sinclair, and Ida Tarbell), that were focused on incredibly detail-oriented articles, making sure to verify details, and seek out as many witnesses to fully comprehend the story. They would write about pertinent social issues in their day, and would create change through their investigative journalism.

PHOTO GALLERY

Ida Tarbell, standing in front of her Twin Oaks home in Easton, Connecticut. The photo dates back to November, 1915.

Ida Tarbell at her Twin Oaks forty-acre farm, located in Easton, Connecticut. The Photo is dated November, 1915.

Ida M. Tarbell's gravestone, located at Woodlawn Cemetery, in Titusville, Pennsylvania.

Portrait of Ida Tarbell.

Ida Tarbell at eight years old.

The Tarbell residence, in Titusville.

Ida Tarbell portrait, from 1917.

Franklin Tarbell, and Ida Tarbell.

Portrait of Ida Tarbell, dating back to 1904.

Portrait of John D. Rockefeller, dated 1895.

John D. Rockefeller (sitting in the chair, with dark clothing and a large hat), as he visited the Pennsylvania oil wells.

This photo of Ida Tarbell, was taken after she had graduated from Allegheny College in 1880. Tarbell was the only female student in her class.

Samuel McClure, of McClure's magazine, where Tarbell worked for a number of years.

Ida Tarbell, left, started to work for the Chautauquan as a female reporter. This photo shows Tarbell posing with a group of female staff members, in 1888.

It is believed that this portrait of Ida Tarbell was taken in 1898.

Ida Tarbell, at her New York desk, working on her McClure's Magazine articles.

Samuel McClure, the man behind the McClure's Magazine where Ida Tarbell would work for years as a journalist.

Ida Tarbell, in 1904, after her book about Standard Oil, and Rockefeller was published.

A Pennsylvania oil field, in 1862.

Ida Tarbell hard at work, in 1905.

www.ingramcontent.com/pod-product-compliance
Lightning Source LLC
Chambersburg PA
CBHW050550160726
48003CB00002B/828